Ron Popeil's

ROTISSERIE &BBQ

Recipe Collection

No portion of this book may be
reproduced by any means without
permission in writing by the publisher.

Printed in the Republic of Korea

ISBN #0-9669118-0-6

For inquiries contact:

IN YOUR KITCHEN BOOKS™

P.O. Box 4719 • Chatsworth, CA 91313-4719

Order From 888-838-0996

Copyright © 1998 by In Your Kitchen Books. All rights reserved

ROTISSERIE
&BBQ

Recipe Collection

ROTISSERIE & BBQ
Recipe Collection

ROTISSERIE &BBQ
Recipe Collection

ROTISSERIE & BBQ
Recipe Collection

Recipe Collection

INTRODUCTION

Recipe Collection

Now you can "Cut the Fat" at home and make your food taste better! Rotisserie food is easy, simple and can be prepared by anyone – whether you consider yourself a "cook" or not.

As the horizontal rotisserie turns, you can almost taste the difference. You watch meats self-baste in their own juices as they rotate. The results are crispy and brown on the outside while juicy and tender inside.

Roasting is the oldest and simplest method of food preparation. Any turning spit that was ever used by primitive man to cook the day's hunt over a campfire was rotisserie cooking. So were the spits that stood near, or in, the fireplaces of castles and inns from the Middle Ages on. Before electricity, the turning of the horizontal spit over an open fire was the preferred way of cooking meats. Now you can experience that simplicity and ease of rotating on a spit right in your own kitchen. Compared with conventional ovens, the horizontal rotisserie keeps the juices in motion so meats won't dry out.

No vertical rotisseries please. Vertical rotisseries allow the juices and fat to gather at the bottom of the food due to gravity. The top parts become dry and bland. That's why continuous rotating of a horizontal spit is important to good cooking.

Not too fast. A spit is just right when it continuously allows the food to be exposed to the heat source – at a rate that also keeps the food from burning. It makes the best tasting food taste better. A lot less fat and more flavor!

Horizontal rotisseries bring out the naturally delicious flavor in foods. But even that can be enhanced with delicious marinades, rubs and BBQ coatings. If marinating for more than a half hour, keep the marinated food in the refrigerator and bring it out 15 minutes prior to placing it on a rotisserie.

You can marinate food for an hour, 4 hours, or even overnight. For speed, use a flavor injector. It works great. Remember to always keep your food cold or hot. That way it stays fresher and retards the growth of unwanted bacteria that promote spoilage.

If your poultry is very cold, wash the cavity with warm water to bring the temperature up before placing it on the spit. Caution: If it is partially frozen on the inside, the inner parts may not become done and there is a risk of uncooked poultry which could carry unwanted bacteria that can make people sick. Use a meat and poultry thermometer to make sure food is cooked the way you want.

Always start with fresh, clean food. When placing wild game on a rotisserie you may find that more aromatic herbs and spices soften some of the "wild" odors. Try garlic, onion and oregano rubs on game. Sage and citrus flavors work well for poultry.

If you are using a self-contained horizontal rotisserie, make sure all the loose parts are tied down securely so they don't come into direct contact with the heat source.

Natural tenderizers. Soy sauce, oil & vinegar, and wine all make natural tenderizers and marinades. Also try orange juice, pineapple juice and lemon/lime citrus juice to help make the food more tender when allowed to marinate for a few hours.

This collection includes recipes that naturally lower fat and will help you enjoy a wide variety of foods with your rotisserie.

HINTS AND TIPS

- When using a rotisserie basket, be sure the top is pressed down firmly to secure the food tightly in place. While rotating, no food should move.
- Trim excess fat and any loose hanging pieces from meats and poultry before placing in a rotisserie.

15

- Once the food is positioned inside a rotisserie, allow it to rotate one time to ensure that nothing hits the heating element or heat reflector.
- Never use an aerosol spray inside a rotisserie or BBQ when operating.
- If you want to check the temperature of the food, manually turn the timer off before opening the door to check the food.
- If you have a "No Heat Rotation" feature, when food is done, set the switch to "No Heat Rotation" and set the timer for 5 minutes and let your food rotate. The meat will be easier to carve and this will allow time for cooling down before removing.
- Parboiling ribs for 15 minutes before putting them on a rotisserie will reduce fat, make them tender and easier to handle.
- To avoid burning, do not baste food with sweet barbeque sauce until approximately 20 minutes before it is done.

COOKING TIMES AND TEMPERATURES

Please note that the times and temperatures at right are only a guide for your reference and are based on temperatures of refrigerated foods. Rotisseries vary and times will vary due to differences in meat shape, size, and amount of fat and bone. To accurately determine whether food is done, insert a meat thermometer into the thickest sections.

FOOD	WEIGHT/QTY.	INTERNAL TEMP.	TIME
CHICKEN			
Whole Chicken	3-1/2 lbs.	180°	15 min./lb.
Cornish Hens(head over heel)	2-4 hens	180°	10 min./lb.
2 Chickens/Ducks		180°	10 min./lb.
Turkey(unstuffed)	12-15 lbs.	180°	12-15 min./lb.
Chicken Pieces			
with bones	3 lbs.	180°	30-35 min. total
without bones	1-1/2 lbs.	180°	30-35 min. total
Turkey Burgers	1-1/4 lbs.	180° well	30-35 min. total
Chicken Kebobs	6 skewers	180° well	30-35 min. total
PORK			
Rolled Pork Loin	3-1/2 lbs.	160°	20-30 min./lb.
Pork Tenderloin	1-3/4 to 2 lbs.	160°	30-35 min./lb.
Pork Chops	4 chops	160°	30-35 min./lb.
Boneless Pork Chops	6 chops	160°	20 min./lb.
Boneless Ham	3 lbs.	160°	45 min./lb.
Italian Sausages			
unrotated	up to 20		30-35 min./lb.
rotated	up to 20		20-25 min./lb.
Hot Dogs	up to 20		10-15 min./lb.
BEEF			
Standing Rib Roast	6 lbs.	160° medium	18 min./lb.
Rolled Rib Roast	4 lbs.	140° rare	16 min./lb.
		160° medium	18 min./lb.
		170° well	20 min./lb.
Steaks	1-1/4 inch	medium	25 min. total
Hamburgers (9)	1/4 lb. each	medium-well	20-30 min. total
Beef Kebobs	6 skewers	medium	20-25 min. total
LAMB			
Leg of Lamb	4-1/2 to 7 lbs.	160° medium	22 min./lb.
SEAFOOD			
Salmon Steaks (In Basket)	4 steaks, 1-1/4 inch		20 min. total
Fish Fillets (In Basket)	3/4 inch		25min. total
Shrimp Kebobs	6 kebobs		25 min. total
Halibut Fillets (In Basket)	3/4 inch (breaded w/dill)		30 min. total
Baked Potato(s)	On Spit Rods		45 minutes

Recipe Collection

ROTISSERIE & BBQ
Recipe Collection

APPETIZERS

ROTISSERIE &BBQ

Recipe Collection

ROASTED VEGETABLE SALSA

Makes 2 cups.

**1 medium red onion, peeled
and halved crosswise
1 red bell pepper, quartered and seeded
1 green bell pepper, quartered and seeded
2 jalapeno chilies, halved and seeded
2 tablespoons olive oil
2 large tomatoes, seeded and chopped
1 teaspoon chili powder
1/8 teaspoon ground cumin
1 tablespoon fresh lime juice
Salt to taste
Tortilla chips**

Brush onion, bell peppers and jalapenos with the olive oil. Place in the basket and rotate for 15 to 20 minutes or until vegetables are tender. Remove vegetables from basket and coarsely chop.

Toss chopped vegetables with tomatoes, chili powder, cumin, lime juice and salt to taste. Let stand at room temperature for 30 minutes before serving with chips for dipping.

ROASTED RED BELL PEPPER DIP

Makes 2 cups.

**3 large red bell peppers
1 green onion, cut into 1-inch pieces
1-1/2 tablespoons lemon juice
1 cup whipped cream cheese
Baguette slices**

Cut the peppers into quarters and remove all the seeds. Place peppers in basket and rotate for 20 minutes or until nicely browned. Remove peppers and place in a paper bag for 10 minutes to steam. Peel off skins.

Place peeled peppers, green onion and lemon juice in the food processor; puree. Add the cream cheese and pulse to mix in. Transfer to a bowl, cover and refrigerate for at least one hour and up to 2 days. Serve to spread on baguette slices.

ROASTED GARLIC DIP

Makes 1 cup.

1 bulb roasted garlic (see page 185)
1/2 cup plain yogurt
1/2 cup mayonnaise
1 tablespoon chopped fresh chives
or green onions
Salt and pepper to taste
Vegetables, chips or crackers

Squeeze garlic from bulb and mash. Stir in yogurt, mayonnaise, chives, salt and pepper to taste. Mix well. Refrigerate, covered, for 2 to 3 hours before serving. Serve with vegetables, chips or crackers for dipping.

ROASTED GARLIC CHEESE TOASTS

Makes 12 pieces.

2 tablespoons olive oil
12 slices (1/4-inch thick) baguette
1/2 cup freshly grated Parmesan cheese
2 heads roasted garlic (see page 185)
2 tablespoons minced chives

Brush one side of the baguette slices with the olive oil and dip into grated Parmesan. Arrange bread in greased basket and rotate until bread is crisp, about 8 to 10 minutes.

Squeeze roasted garlic from bulb and mash well. Spread garlic on the toasts and top with chives. Serve as appetizers or with soup or salad.

BRUSCHETTA

Garlic Bread topped with Tomatoes and Fresh Basil

Makes 8 pieces.

**4 slices (1-inch thick) Italian
or French bread
2 cloves garlic, minced
6 tablespoons olive oil, divided use
3 large tomatoes, seeded and chopped
2 tablespoons minced fresh basil
1 tablespoon balsamic or red wine vinegar
Salt and pepper to taste**

Combine garlic and 4 tablespoons olive oil in a small bowl. Let stand several hours to flavor the oil. Toss together the tomatoes, basil, remaining garlic, oil, balsamic or red wine vinegar, and salt and pepper to taste. Let stand at room temperature for 30 to 60 minutes.

Brush the oil on both cut sides of the bread. Place bread in the basket and rotate until bread is toasted, about 10 minutes. Remove bread to a serving plate and cut in half on the diagonal. Mound the tomato salad on the bread and serve immediately.

ROTISSERIE
&BBQ
Recipe Collection

ROASTED SPICY
CHICKEN QUESADILLA WEDGES

Serves 8.

1/2 recipe Pollo Asado (see page 72)
8 (10-inch) flour tortillas
2 tablespoons vegetable oil
1 cup grated medium sharp Cheddar cheese
1 cup grated Monterey Jack cheese
1/2 cup crumbled goat cheese
3 tablespoons chopped fresh cilantro

Prepare chicken as directed and cool slightly. Cut chicken into small shreds or cubes. Brush one side of each tortilla with oil. Lay 4 of the tortillas, oil side down, on a baking sheet. Divide chicken evenly over the tortillas. Top with cheeses and cilantro. Next, lay the remaining 4 tortillas, oil side up, on top. Wrap well and refrigerate until ready to cook.

Preheat oven to 400 degrees. Bake the quesadillas until crispy and browned, about 12 to 15 minutes. Cut each into six wedges and serve hot or warm.

ROASTED EGGPLANT DIP
WITH FRESH DILL

Makes 2 cups.

1 large eggplant
2 tablespoons olive oil, divided use
1 tablespoon fresh lemon juice
1 clove garlic, minced
1 to 2 tablespoons minced fresh dill
Salt and pepper to taste
Paprika
Warmed pita bread wedges

Cut eggplant in half lengthwise and brush cut surfaces with 1 tablespoon olive oil. Place in basket and rotate for 30 to 40 minutes or until the eggplant is very soft. Scrape the eggplant pulp out of the skin into a food processor or blender container. Add the remaining 1 tablespoon olive oil, the lemon juice, garlic and dill. Season to taste with salt and pepper. Sprinkle with paprika and serve with pita wedges.

Tip: To warm pita bread, wrap in foil in place in steamer tray to warm for the last 10 minutes of the eggplant rotating time.

EGGPLANT CAVIAR

Makes 2 cups.

1 large eggplant
3 tablespoons olive oil, divided use
1 medium tomato, seeded and chopped
1/4 cup diced green onions
1/2 cup diced green or yellow bell pepper
3 tablespoons sliced black ripe olives
1-1/2 tablespoons fresh lemon juice
Salt and pepper to taste
Warmed pita bread wedges

Cut the eggplant in half lengthwise and brush the cut surfaces with 1 tablespoon olive oil. Place in basket and rotate for 30 to 40 minutes or until the eggplant is very soft. Scrape the eggplant pulp out of the skin into a bowl. Chop the eggplant pulp and stir in the remaining 2 tablespoons olive oil, tomato, green onions, bell pepper, olives. lemon juice, salt and pepper to taste. Serve with pita wedges.

Tip: To warm pita bread, wrap in foil and place in steamer tray to warm for the last 10 minutes of the eggplant rotating time.

RON'S SPICY CHICKEN WINGS

Makes 10 to 14.

2 eggs, slightly beaten
1 tablespoon water
1 cup plain dry breadcrumbs
2 tablespoons Dijon mustard
1 tablespoon lemon pepper
1 teaspoon cayenne pepper
14 chicken drummettes
or 10 chicken wings

Combine eggs and mustard in a flat dish. Toss together the breadcrumbs, lemon pepper, and cayenne pepper in another flat dish on a sheet of wax paper.

Wash and thoroughly dry the chicken wings. Dip chicken in the egg to coat well and then dredge in the breadcrumbs to make a thick crust.

Rotate the chicken wings in the 1-inch basket for 45 minutes or until they are browned and cooked through.

CAJUN CHICKEN WINGS

Makes 14.

14 chicken drummettes
4 tablespoons melted butter
Cajun-Creole Spice Rub (See page 236)

Wash and thoroughly dry the chicken drummettes. Dip chicken in melted butter to coat thoroughly and then coat well with Cajun-Creole Rub. Rotate the chicken wings in the Flat Standard Basket for 45 minutes or until they are browned and cooked through.

SPICY PEANUT DRUMMETTES

Makes 28.

**28 chicken drummettes
1/4 cup creamy peanut butter
1/4 cup soy sauce
3 tablespoons honey
2 cloves garlic, minced
1/2 teaspoon hot red pepper flakes
1/3 cup finely chopped roasted peanuts
1/2 cup finely chopped fresh cilantro**

Rotate the chicken wings in the Flat Standard Basket for 45 minutes or until they are browned and cooked through.

Meanwhile, heat the peanut butter, soy sauce, honey, garlic and red pepper flakes in a small saucepan over low heat until smooth. Toss with hot cooked wings and transfer to a serving dish. Sprinkle with peanuts and cilantro.

MAHOGANY CHICKEN WINGS

Makes 10 to 14.

**1/4 cup honey
3 tablespoons soy sauce
2 tablespoons Hoisin sauce
1 teaspoon grated orange rind
1 clove garlic, minced
14 chicken drummettes
or 10 chicken wings**

In a food storage bag or a glass, plastic or stainless bowl combine the honey, soy sauce, Hoisin sauce, orange rind and garlic. Blend well.

Wash and thoroughly dry the chicken wings and add to the marinade. Seal the bag or bowl and refrigerate for 6 hours or overnight, turning occasionally.

Remove the wings from the marinade reserving the marinade for basting. Rotate the chicken wings in the Flat Standard Basket for 45 minutes or until they are browned and cooked through, basting with reserved marinade during the last 10 minutes.

PORK SATAY WITH PEANUT SAUCE

Serves 6.

MARINADE:
1 tablespoon brown sugar
1 tablespoon curry powder
2 tablespoons crunchy peanut butter
1/2 cup soy sauce
1/2 cup freshly squeezed lime juice
2 cloves garlic, minced

2 pork tenderloins
(about 1-1/2 to 2 pounds total)
Peanut Dipping Sauce (see page 231)

For the marinade, combine the brown sugar, curry powder, peanut butter, soy sauce, lime juice and garlic in a shallow dish. Trim the pork of all fat and silverskin. Cut pork into 1-inch cubes. Place the pork in the marinade and let stand for 2 to 8 hours, covered, in the refrigerator.

When ready to rotate, thread pork on skewers. Rotate the kebobs for 25 to 30 minutes or until cooked to desired doneness. Remove pork to serving plates.

Place the Peanut Dipping Sauce in the warming tray in the lower position. Serve sauce warm with pork.

Tip: Substitute a prepared Peanut Sauce, if desired.

TANDOORI SHRIMP

Serves 6.

**2 pounds extra-large raw shrimp, cleaned
1 teaspoon ground coriander
1 teaspoon ground cumin
1/2 cup plain yogurt
2 tablespoons fresh lemon juice
1/2 cup finely chopped onion
1 teaspoon minced garlic
1 teaspoon paprika
1/2 teaspoon ground turmeric
1/2 teaspoon salt
1/4 teaspoon freshly ground pepper**

Place cleaned shrimp in a glass or stainless steel bowl. Place coriander and cumin in a small skillet over medium heat and toast for about 2 minutes, tossing often until fragrant. Cool.

To the shrimp add the cooled spices, yogurt, lemon juice, onion, garlic, paprika, turmeric, salt and pepper. Stir to combine well. Cover and refrigerate for no longer than 4 hours.

Skewer shrimp and rotate for 15 minutes or until shrimp turn bright orange in color. Remove skewers from the gear wheels and slide the shrimp off onto serving plates.

MARTINI SHRIMP

Serves 8.

**1/2 cup dry vermouth
1/4 cup olive oil
1/4 cup chopped onion
1/4 cup lemon juice
2 tablespoons chopped fresh parsley
1 tablespoon white wine
Worcestershire sauce
2 cloves garlic, minced
1/2 teaspoon salt
1/2 teaspoon pepper
2 pounds extra-large shrimp, cleaned**

In a shallow glass or stainless steel bowl stir together the vermouth, olive oil, onion, lemon juice, fresh parsley, white wine, Worcestershire, garlic, salt and pepper. Toss the shrimp in the marinade. Cover and refrigerate for up to 4 hours.

Skewer shrimp and rotate for 15 minutes or until shrimp turn bright orange in color. Remove skewers from the gear wheels and slide the shrimp off onto serving plates.

BREADED SEA SCALLOPS

Makes 21.

**1 cup flour
1 tablespoon paprika
1 teaspoon salt
1 teaspoon freshly ground pepper
1 teaspoon garlic powder
1 egg beaten
1 cup milk
1 cup plain dry breadcrumbs
21 sea scallops
Tartar sauce or Cocktail sauce**

Combine flour, paprika, salt, pepper and garlic powder in a shallow dish. Whisk egg and milk together in a shallow bowl. Place breadcrumbs in a third dish.

Dredge scallops in flour mixture, then dip in egg and finally coat well with breadcrumbs. Place in the greased basket and rotate for about 20 minutes or until just cooked through and firm. Serve with choice of sauce.

APPETIZERS

ROTISSERIE & BBQ

Recipe Collection

ROTISSERIE & BBQ

Recipe Collection

SALADS

ROASTED PEPPER AND EGGPLANT SALAD

Serves 4.

**4 small Japanese eggplants,
cut in half lengthwise
1 small red onion, peeled and cut in half
1 medium red bell pepper,
cut in half and seeded
6 teaspoons olive oil, divided use
1/4 cup crumbled feta cheese
3 teaspoons balsamic vinegar
1 teaspoon fresh lemon juice
1/4 teaspoon Dijon mustard
1 clove garlic, minced
2 teaspoons minced fresh basil leaves**

Brush the eggplant, red onion and red bell pepper with some of the olive oil and place in the basket. Roast for 15 to 20 minutes or until lightly browned. Arrange the eggplant around the edge of a platter. Separate the onion rings and place in the center of the platter. Cut the peppers into strips and place around the onions. Sprinkle with feta cheese.

To make the dressing, whisk the remaining olive oil, balsamic, lemon juice, mustard, garlic and minced basil in a small bowl. Pour over the salad and serve immediately.

ROASTED RED POTATO SALAD WITH HERB VINAIGRETTE

Serves 8.

1-1/2 lb. whole tiny new potatoes, quartered
3 teaspoons olive oil
2 cloves garlic, minced
4 teaspoons minced fresh rosemary
Salt and pepper
1 (6 ounce) can pitted ripe olives, cut in half
1 yellow bell pepper, diced
12 cherry tomatoes, cut in half

HERB VINAIGRETTE:
1/3 cup olive oil
1/3 cup white wine vinegar
1/2 teaspoon dried thyme
1 teaspoon sugar
1 teaspoon Dijon mustard
Salt and pepper

Combine oil, garlic, rosemary, 1/2 teaspoon salt and 1/4 teaspoon pepper in a small bowl. Drizzle over potatoes; toss gently to coat. Place potatoes in the basket and roast for 30 to 40 minutes or until tender.

In a large bowl combine the olives, yellow pepper and tomatoes. Add the potatoes. Whisk the Herb Vinaigrette ingredients together and toss with salad. Serve warm or cover and chill for up to 24 hours.

41

CHICKEN CAESAR SALAD

Serves 4.

**4 boneless chicken breast halves
6 teaspoons olive oil
6 teaspoons canola oil
4 teaspoons lemon juice
2 garlic cloves, minced
2 teaspoons Worcestershire sauce
1/4 cup freshly grated Parmesan cheese
Salt and pepper to taste
1 medium head romaine lettuce,
torn into small pieces
1 cup Garlic Cheese croutons
Coarsely grated fresh Parmesan cheese**

Wash and pat dry chicken breasts and pound between two sheets of plastic wrap to a thickness of 1/2 inch. Whisk together the oils, lemon juice, garlic, Worcestershire sauce and 1/4 cup Parmesan.

Brush the chicken with some of the dressing. Place the chicken in the basket and roast for 12 to 15 minutes or until cooked through. Remove chicken and cut crosswise into thick strips.

Toss the lettuce with the remaining dressing, the croutons and the coarsely grated Parmesan. Divide evenly on four plates and top with chicken.

BBQ CHICKEN SALAD

Serves 4.

1 rotated BBQ chicken (see page 56), chilled
1/2 cup chopped celery
1/2 cup chopped red bell pepper
1/4 cup chopped red onion
1/2 cup mayonnaise
4 teaspoons Tomato BBQ Sauce
(see page 219)
4 lettuce leaves

Shred the chilled rotated chicken and toss with celery, red pepper, and onion. Stir together the mayonnaise and BBQ sauce and toss with the chicken salad. Chill until ready to serve, up to 4 hours. Mound on lettuce leaves to serve.

SOUTHWESTERN CHICKEN SALAD

Serves 6.

4 chicken breasts
Southwestern Rub (see page 237)
1 cup diced celery
1/2 cup chopped red bell pepper
1/2 cup sliced black olives
1 (4 ounce) can diced green chilies
1/4 cup diced green onions
3 teaspoons fresh lemon juice
3 cups shredded fresh spinach
1/4 cup toasted pine nuts or almonds

DRESSING:
1 cup mayonnaise
1/4 cup sour cream or yogurt
1 teaspoon Dijon mustard
1/2 teaspoon salt
1/8 teaspoon cayenne pepper
1/8 teaspoon freshly ground pepper

Wash and pat dry the chicken--you may remove the skin, if you wish. Completely coat the chicken with the Southwestern Rub. Place chicken pieces in the basket and rotate for 30 to 40 minutes or until cooked through. Cool chicken and then shred or dice.

Toss the chicken, celery, red pepper, olives, chilies, green onions and lemon juice together in a large bowl. Cover and refrigerate until 1 hour before serving.

Stir together all the dressing ingredients and toss with salad. Mound chicken salad on the shredded spinach and sprinkle with toasted nuts.

ROTISSERIE & BBQ

Recipe Collection

ASIAN BEEF SALAD

Serves 4 as main course.

1 pound beef sirloin
Salt and pepper
1/4 cup vegetable oil
2 teaspoons Asian sesame oil
1 teaspoon hot chili sauce or to taste
2 teaspoons soy sauce
2 teaspoons rice vinegar
1 teaspoon freshly squeezed lemon juice
2 teaspoons minced fresh cilantro
1 teaspoon minced fresh ginger root
2 teaspoons orange zest
1 teaspoon minced garlic
1 carrot, peeled & cut julienne
1 red bell pepper, cut very thin julienne
1/2 red onion, thinly sliced in half rings
1 cup fresh watercress or cilantro sprigs
1 bunch fresh spinach, washed,
trimmed and chilled

Season the steak with salt and pepper. Place the steak in the basket and rotate for 15 minutes for rare or 20 minutes for medium. Remove steak and slice thinly across the grain.

To make the dressing, combine the oil, sesame oil, chili sauce, soy sauce, vinegar, lemon juice, cilantro, ginger, orange zest and garlic in a bowl and whisk to blend well. Add the beef strips and let stand for about 15 minutes.

46

Just before serving, remove the beef from the dressing with a slotted utensil, reserving dressing. Combine the beef, carrot, red pepper, onion, watercress or cilantro, mint and spinach in a large bowl. Add reserved dressing to taste and toss to coat all ingredients. Serve immediately.

PORK AND BEAN SALAD

Serves 4.

**1 rotated Pork Tenderloin
with Spicy Texas Rub (see page 91)
1/2 cup oil and vinegar salad dressing
2 teaspoons ketchup
1/2 teaspoon chili powder
1/4 teaspoon ground cumin
1 (15 ounce) can black beans,
rinsed and drained
1 (15 ounce) can kidney beans,
rinsed and drained
1 cup fresh or frozen corn kernels
1 cup diced fresh tomato
1 green bell pepper, diced
1/4 cup diced red onion
1/4 cup chopped fresh cilantro or parsley
6 cups mixed lettuce greens
1 cup slightly crushed corn chips**

Cut the rotated pork into strips and place in a large bowl. Whisk together the salad dressing, ketchup, chili powder and cumin. Toss with pork and set aside while preparing the remaining ingredients.

Toss together the beans, corn, tomato, green pepper, onion and cilantro. Add to the pork and toss well. Arrange a bed of lettuce on serving plates and top with pork salad. Garnish with corn chips.

TANDOORI SHRIMP SALAD WITH CURRY VINAIGRETTE

Serves 4.

**1 recipe Tandoori Shrimp (see page 34)
8 cups mixed salad greens
2 large tomatoes, cut in wedges
2 carrots, cut into strips
2 stalks celery, cut into strips**

**CURRY VINAIGRETTE:
1/2 cup olive oil
1/4 cup red wine vinegar
2 tablespoons minced green onions
1 teaspoon minced fresh garlic
1 tablespoon curry powder
1 tablespoon brown sugar
Salt and pepper to taste**

Prepare the Tandoori Shrimp. Meanwhile, prepare the vinaigrette by whisking together all ingredients. Toss the salad greens with 1/4 cup of the vinaigrette. Mound the lettuce on serving plates. Top with Tandoori shrimp, tomatoes, carrots and celery. Drizzle more dressing to taste over all.

WATERCRESS AND SCALLOP SALAD WITH CITRUS VINAIGRETTE

Serves 4.

CITRUS VINAIGRETTE:
1/3 cup fresh orange juice
1/3 cup white wine vinegar
2 teaspoons chopped fresh basil
1 teaspoon fresh lemon juice
1 teaspoon grated orange zest
1/2 teaspoon grated lemon zest
2 teaspoons olive oil

1-1/2 pounds sea scallops, patted dry
4 cups watercress leaves
4 cups baby spinach leaves
2 carrots, cut in thin strips

To make the Citrus Vinaigrette, whisk all the ingredients together in a small bowl. Remove 1/4 cup of the vinaigrette and pour over the scallops. Refrigerate for 10 minutes.

Place scallops in basket and rotate for 12 to 15 minutes or until just done. Meanwhile, toss together the watercress and spinach with the remaining vinaigrette. Mound greens on serving plates and toss with hot scallops and carrots. Serve immediately.

ASIAN FRESH TUNA SALAD

Serves 4.

Asian Citrus Marinade (see page 210)
1-1/4 pound tuna steaks, cut 3/4-inch thick
4 cups shredded Napa cabbage
4 cups shredded red leaf lettuce
2 carrots, cut in thin strips
2 cups bean sprouts, rinsed and drained
2 teaspoons toasted sesame seeds

Prepare the Asian Citrus Marinade and pour half over the tuna steaks. Refrigerate to marinate for 10 minutes to 1 hour.

Place the tuna in the basket and rotate in the stopped position facing the heat rods for 4 minutes. Turn basket and rotate the other side of the tuna for 4 minutes. It should be slightly pink in the center when tested.

Toss the cabbage, lettuce, carrots, and bean sprouts with the remaining marinade. Divide evenly on serving plates and top with tuna. Sprinkle with sesame seeds and serve.

Recipe Collection

ROTISSERIE &BBQ
Recipe Collection

POULTRY

Recipe Collection

ROAST CHICKEN WITH LEMON HERB RUB

Serves 3 to 4.

**Minced rind of 2 lemons
5 cloves garlic, minced
1 tablespoon dried thyme, finely crumbled
2 teaspoons dried rosemary,
finely crumbled
2 teaspoons dried sage leaves,
finely crumbled
1 3-1/2 to 4 pound whole chicken
Salt and freshly ground pepper**

In a small bowl or with a mortar and pestle combine lemon, garlic, and herbs to form a slightly moist paste.

Wash the chicken and dry thoroughly, inside and out. Loosen the skin across the breast and then down around the leg and thigh using a chop stick or your fingers. Work the seasoning mixture under the skin and into the meat of the breasts, legs and thighs and all over the outside skin as well. Season the cavity of the chicken with salt and pepper. Using an elastic food tie, truss the chicken.

Rotate the chicken on the spit rods for 55 to 60 minutes or until the internal temperature reaches 170 degrees on the instant thermometer inserted in the thigh meat. Remove chicken and cut into pieces to serve.

BBQ CHICKEN

Serves 3 to 4.

1 3-1/2 to 4 pound whole chicken
1/2 cup Tomato BBQ or Chipotle BBQ Sauce
(see pages 219 and 220)

Wash the chicken and dry thoroughly, inside and out. Season the cavity of the chicken with salt and pepper. Using an elastic food tie, truss the chicken.

Rotate the chicken on the spit rods for 45 minutes. Brush some of the BBQ sauce all over the outside of the chicken. Continue rotating 10 to 15 minutes longer or until the internal temperature reaches 170 degrees on the instant thermometer inserted in the thigh meat. Remove chicken and cut into pieces to serve.

ROAST CHICKEN WITH CHERRY BRANDY SAUCE

Serves 3 to 4.

**2 tablespoons butter, melted
1 teaspoon soy sauce
1/2 teaspoon ground ginger
1/2 teaspoon paprika
1/2 teaspoon salt
1/8 teaspoon freshly ground pepper
1 3-1/2 to 4 pound whole chicken
1-1/2 cups Cherry Brandy Sauce
(see page 225)**

Stir together the butter, soy sauce, ginger, paprika, salt and pepper. Wash the chicken and dry thoroughly, inside and out. Loosen the skin across the breast and then down around the leg and thigh using a chop stick or your fingers. Work the butter mixture under the skin and into the meat of the breasts, legs and thighs and all over the outside skin as well. Season the cavity of the chicken with salt and pepper. Using an elastic food tie, truss the chicken.

Rotate the chicken on the spit rods for 55 to 60 minutes or until the internal temperature reaches 170 degrees on the instant thermometer inserted in the thigh meat. Remove chicken and cut into pieces to serve with warm Cherry Brandy Sauce.

TERIYAKI ROAST CHICKEN

Serves 3 to 4.

GINGER TERIYAKI SAUCE:
1/2 cup soy sauce
1/2 cup dry white wine
1/4 cup sake or dry sherry
1/4 cup sugar
2 slices fresh ginger root
2 tablespoons water
1 tablespoon cornstarch

1 3-1/2 to 4 pound whole chicken

To prepare Ginger Teriyaki Sauce combine the soy sauce, wine, sake or sherry, sugar and ginger in a small saucepan. Bring to a boil and then simmer over medium heat 3 minutes. Blend water with cornstarch; stir into sauce. Stir over medium heat 1 minute or until thickened. Strain sauce. Makes about 1 cup. Set aside to cool or refrigerate up to 1 week.

Wash the chicken and dry thoroughly, inside and out. Loosen the skin across the breast and then down around the leg and thigh using a chop stick or your fingers. Reserve 1/2 cup of the cooled teriyaki sauce and pour some of the remaining sauce under the skin of the chicken and work it over the breast, legs and thighs. Rub more of the sauce all over the outside of the chicken. Let the chicken marinate for 30 minutes.

Rotate the chicken on the spit rods for 55 to 60 minutes or until the internal temperature reaches 170 degrees on the instant thermometer inserted in the thigh meat. Remove chicken and cut into pieces to serve. Serve the chicken with the remaining teriyaki sauce for dipping.

Tip: You may substitute a prepared Teriyaki Marinade for the Ginger Teriyaki Sauce in this recipe.

GARLIC BASIL ROAST CHICKEN

Serves 3 to 4.

3 cloves garlic, peeled
1/4 cup fresh basil leaves
1 tablespoon olive oil
Salt and pepper
1 3-1/2 to 4 pound whole chicken

In the food processor or with a mortar and pestle, finely mash the garlic with the fresh basil and olive oil to make a paste. Season with salt and pepper.

Wash the chicken and dry thoroughly, inside and out. Loosen the skin across the breast and then down around the leg and thigh using a chop stick or your fingers. Work the garlic-basil seasoning mixture under the skin and into the meat of the breasts, legs and thighs and all over the outside skin as well. Season the cavity of the chicken with salt and pepper. Using an elastic food tie, truss the chicken.

Rotate the chicken on the spit rods for 55 to 60 minutes or until the internal temperature reaches 170 degrees on the instant thermometer inserted in the thigh meat. Remove chicken and cut into pieces to serve.

PESTO RUBBED ROAST CHICKEN

Serves 3 to 4.

1 recipe Basil Pesto Rub (See page 240)
1 3-1/2 pound whole chicken

Prepare the Basil Pesto Rub. Wash the chicken and dry thoroughly, inside and out. Loosen the skin across the breast and then down around the leg and thigh using a chop stick or your fingers. Work the pesto under the skin and into the meat of the breasts, legs and thighs and all over the outside skin as well. Season the cavity of the chicken with salt and pepper. Using an elastic food tie, truss the chicken.

Rotate the chicken on the spit rods for 55 to 60 minutes or until the internal temperature reaches 170 degrees on the instant thermometer inserted in the thigh meat. Remove chicken and cut into pieces to serve.

OVEN-FRIED
CHICKEN PARMESAN PIECES

Serves 3 to 4.

**3 eggs, slightly beaten
1 tablespoon water
1 teaspoon Dijon mustard
2 cups seasoned dry breadcrumbs
1/2 cup freshly grated Parmesan cheese
1/2 teaspoon paprika
1 3 pound chicken, cut into serving pieces
or 4 chicken breasts**

Combine eggs and mustard in a flat dish. Toss together the breadcrumbs, Parmesan cheese and paprika in another flat dish or on a sheet of wax paper.

Wash and thoroughly dry the chicken pieces. Dip chicken pieces in the egg to coat well and then dredge in the breadcrumbs to make a thick crust.

Rotate the chicken in the Flat Standard Basket for 45 minutes or until lightly browned and cooked through.

ROSEMARY-SCENTED CHICKEN BREASTS

Serves 6.

**2 cloves garlic, minced
1 tablespoon fresh rosemary, minced
1/4 cup olive oil
3 tablespoons balsamic vinegar
Salt and pepper
6 chicken breast halves**

Stir together the garlic, rosemary, olive oil and balsamic. Season with salt and pepper. Wash and thoroughly dry the chicken breasts and add to the marinade, turning to coat well. Cover and refrigerate 3 to 4 hours.

Rotate the chicken breasts in the Flat Standard Basket for 45 minutes or until nicely browned and cooked through.

THAI MARINATED CHICKEN PIECES
WITH
ASIAN SWEET-SPICY DIPPING SAUCE

Serves 3 to 4.

**8 cloves garlic, peeled
2 tablespoons chopped fresh cilantro
2 tablespoons soy sauce
1 tablespoon vegetable oil
Salt and pepper
3 pounds chicken thighs
Asian Sweet-Spicy Dipping Sauce
(see page 230)**

In a food processor or blender combine the garlic, cilantro, soy sauce, oil, salt and pepper to taste and puree. Transfer the sauce to a large bowl.

Wash and thoroughly dry the chicken thighs. Add to the marinade in the bowl and toss to coat well. Cover and refrigerate for 1 to 24 hours. Rotate the chicken in the Flat Standard Basket for 45 minutes or until browned and cooked through. Serve with Asian Sweet-Spicy Dipping Sauce.

TANDOORI CHICKEN BREASTS

Serves 6.

1/2 cup plain yogurt
4 cloves garlic, minced
1 tablespoon fresh ginger root, minced
1/2 cup fresh lime juice
1-1/2 tablespoons ground coriander
1 teaspoon ground cumin
1/2 teaspoon paprika
1/2 teaspoon cayenne pepper
1/4 teaspoon turmeric
Salt and pepper
6 chicken breasts halves

Combine yogurt, garlic, ginger, lime juice and spices in a large bowl. Wash and thoroughly dry the chicken breasts. Add to the yogurt mixture; toss to coat well. Cover and refrigerate 12 to 24 hours.

Rotate the chicken in the Flat Standard Basket for 45 minutes or until browned and cooked through.

HONEY MUSTARD CHICKEN BREASTS

Serves 6.

**1/2 cup honey
1/4 cup Dijon mustard
2 tablespoons vegetable oil
1 teaspoon curry powder
1 teaspoon salt
6 chicken breast halves**

In a shallow baking dish stir together the honey, mustard, oil, curry powder and salt. Wash and pat dry the chicken pieces and coat well with the honey-mustard mixture. Cover and refrigerate for at least 1 hour or up to 24 hours.

Rotate the chicken in the Flat Standard Basket for 45 minutes or until browned and cooked through.

SOUTHWESTERN TACO CHICKEN PIECES WITH LIME-CHILI MARINADE

Serves 4.

Lime Chili Marinade (see page 212)
1 3-1/2 to 4 pound chicken, cut into pieces
3/4 cup flour
1 (1 ounce) envelope Taco seasoning mix
2 eggs beaten with 2 tablespoons water

Prepare the marinade in a large bowl. Wash and thoroughly dry the chicken pieces. Add to the marinade and toss to coat well. Cover and refrigerate for 1 to 4 hours.

Toss the flour and Taco seasoning mix together on a plate. Dip the chicken in the beaten egg mixture and coat well with taco-flour mixture. Rotate the chicken in the Flat Standard Basket for 45 minutes or until browned and cooked through.

Tip: You may skip the marinating in this recipe and simply coat the chicken in egg and the taco-flour mixture before rotating.

CUBAN CHICKEN WITH MOJO MARINADE

Serves 6.

Cuban Mojo Marinade (see page 213)
6 chicken breast halves

Prepare the Mojo Marinade and place in a large bowl. Wash and thoroughly dry the chicken breasts and add to the marinade. Toss to coat well. Cover and refrigerate for 1 to 3 hours.

Rotate the chicken in the Flat Standard Basket for 45 minutes or until lightly browned and cooked through.

PECAN-CRUSTED BONELESS CHICKEN BREASTS

Serves 6.

6 skinless boneless chicken breast halves
1/2 cup Dijon mustard
2 eggs
1/2 cup finely chopped toasted pecans
1-1/2 cups plain dry bread crumbs

Wash and thoroughly pat dry the chicken breasts. Pound the chicken breasts lightly between two sheets of plastic wrap with a flat mallet until they are 1/2-inch thick. Stir together the mustard and eggs in a flat bowl. Toss together the pecans and bread crumbs in another bowl.

Dip chicken in egg mixture and then coat well with the bread crumbs. Rotate the chicken in the Flat Standard Basket for 20 minutes or until lightly browned and cooked through.

SESAME-CRUSTED
BONELESS CHICKEN BREASTS

Serves 6.

6 skinless boneless chicken breast halves
1/2 cup dry sherry
2 tablespoons soy sauce
1 teaspoon Asian sesame oil
2 teaspoons corn starch
1/2 cup toasted sesame seeds

Wash and thoroughly pat dry the chicken breasts. Pound the chicken breasts lightly between two sheets of plastic wrap with a flat mallet until they are 1/2-inch thick. Combine the sherry, soy, sesame oil and cornstarch in a flat baking dish. Add the chicken and turn to coat well. Let stand for 10 minutes. Remove chicken and coat with sesame seeds.

Rotate the chicken in the Flat Standard Basket for 20 minutes or until lightly browned and cooked through.

DIJON CHICKEN BREASTS

Serves 6.

6 skinless boneless chicken breast halves
1 cup plain dry breadcrumbs
1/2 cup freshly grated Parmesan cheese
2 tablespoons minced fresh parsley
4 tablespoons unsalted butter, melted
2 tablespoons Dijon mustard
1 clove garlic, minced

Wash and thoroughly pat dry the chicken breasts. Pound the chicken breasts lightly between two sheets of plastic wrap with a flat mallet until they are 1/2-inch thick. Toss together the breadcrumbs, Parmesan cheese, and parsley in a shallow dish. Stir garlic and mustard into melted butter.

Dip each chicken breast into the butter mixture and then coat well in with the crumbs. Rotate the chicken in the Flat Standard Basket for 20 minutes or until lightly browned and cooked through.

POLLO ASADO CHICKEN BREASTS

Serves 6.

3/4 cup apple juice
3 tablespoons fresh lime juice
3 cloves garlic, minced
1 serrano or jalapeno chili, minced
1/2 teaspoon paprika
1/2 teaspoon dried oregano
1/2 teaspoon freshly ground pepper
6 skinless boneless chicken breast halves

Combine the apple juice, lime juice, garlic, chili, paprika, oregano and pepper in a flat dish. Wash and thoroughly pat dry the chicken breasts. Pound the chicken breasts lightly between two sheets of plastic wrap with a flat mallet until they are 1/2-inch thick. Add the chicken to the marinade. Cover and refrigerate 1 to 4 hours.

Rotate the chicken in the Flat Standard Basket for 20 minutes or until lightly browned and cooked through.

Tip:. After rotating, chicken my be sliced diagonally and rolled up in tortillas with grated cheese, lettuce, salsa and sour cream.

CHICKEN CORDON BLEU

Serves 6.

**6 skinless boneless chicken breast halves
1 tablespoon Dijon mustard
6 thin slices ham
6 thin slices Swiss cheese
2 eggs beaten with 2 tablespoons water
2 cups Italian seasoned bread crumbs**

Wash and thoroughly pat dry the chicken breasts. Pound the chicken breasts lightly between two sheets of plastic wrap with a flat mallet until they are 1/4-inch thick. Place the breasts smooth side down on a work surface and spread each with 1/2 teaspoon mustard. Top with a slice of ham and cheese. Fold in the sides and roll up the breasts. Secure with a toothpick.

Dip the chicken rolls in the egg mixture and then in the breadcrumbs to coat well. Rotate the chicken in the Flat Standard Basket for 35 to 40 minutes or until lightly browned and cooked through. Remove toothpicks and serve.

CHILI AND CHEESE
STUFFED CHICKEN ROLLS

Serves 6.

6 skinless boneless chicken breast halves
6 whole canned mild chilies
6 slices Jack cheese
2 eggs beaten with 2 tablespoons water
2 cups crushed cheese crackers

Wash and thoroughly pat dry the chicken breasts. Pound the chicken breasts lightly between two sheets of plastic wrap with a flat mallet until they are 1/4-inch thick. Place the breasts smooth side down on a work surface and top with a chili and a slice of cheese. Fold in the sides and roll up the breasts. Secure with a toothpick.

Dip the chicken rolls in the egg mixture and then in the cracker crumbs to coat well. Rotate the chicken in the Flat Standard Basket for 35 to 40 minutes or until lightly browned and cooked through. Remove toothpicks and serve.

SUN-DRIED TOMATO STUFFED POCKET CHICKEN

Serves 6.

**6 skinless boneless chicken breast halves
1/4 cup prepared Pesto sauce
or Basil Pesto Rub (see page 240)
2 tablespoons minced sun-dried tomatoes,
packed in oil
2 tablespoons Parmesan cheese,
freshly grated
2 eggs beaten with 2 tablespoons water
2 cups plain dry breadcrumbs**

Wash and thoroughly pat dry the chicken breasts. Cut a pocket in the side of each chicken breast about 2 inches long. Stir together the pesto, sun-dried tomatoes and Parmesan cheese. Fill the pockets with this mixture and pinch to seal edges or secure with a toothpick.

Dip the chicken rolls in the egg mixture and then in the breadcrumbs to coat well. Rotate the chicken in the Flat Standard Basket for 20 to 25 minutes or until lightly browned and cooked through. Remove any toothpicks and serve.

SOUTHWESTERN POCKET CHICKEN

Serves 6.

6 skinless boneless chicken breast halves
1/4 cup Cilantro Pesto Rub (see page 240)
1/4 cup crumbled soft goat cheese
Southwestern Rub (see page 237)

Wash and thoroughly pat dry the chicken breasts. Cut a pocket in the side of each chicken breast about 2 inches long. Stir together the pesto and goat cheese. Fill the pockets with this mixture and pinch to seal edges or secure with a toothpick.

Dip the chicken rolls in the egg mixture and then coat well with the Southwestern Rub. Rotate the chicken in the Flat Standard Basket for 20 to 25 minutes or until lightly browned and cooked through. Remove any toothpicks and serve.

LEMON CHICKEN KEBOBS

Serves 4 to 8.

**4 skinless boneless chicken breast halves
1 zucchini, cut into 24 (1-inch) rounds
1 red bell pepper,
cut into 24 (1-inch) squares
1 teaspoon grated lemon zest
3 tablespoons fresh lemon juice
1-1/2 teaspoons sugar
3/4 teaspoon dried oregano
Salt and pepper**

Cut the chicken breasts lengthwise into 4 strips. Combine the chicken strips, zucchini, red pepper, lemon zest and juice, sugar, oregano and salt and pepper to taste in a large bowl. Toss to coat well. Cover and let stand 15 minutes.

Thread a zucchini, red pepper, then weave a strip of chicken on a kebob skewer, repeat and then finish with another zucchini and pepper. Repeat 7 more times. Rotate kebobs for 25 to 30 minutes or until the chicken and vegetables are cooked through.

CHICKEN FAJITA SKEWERS

Serves 4 to 6.

1/2 cup fresh lime juice
1/2 cup vegetable oil
1/2 cup beer
1/4 cup brown sugar
1 onion, thinly sliced
1 clove garlic, minced
2 fresh jalapeno chilies, sliced
2 tablespoons ground cumin
2 tablespoons paprika
1 tablespoon Worcestershire sauce
1 teaspoon freshly ground pepper
1-1/2 pounds boneless chicken breasts
8 flour tortillas
Shredded cheese
Shredded lettuce
Sour cream

In a large bowl, combine lime juice, oil, beer, brown sugar, onion, jalapeno, cumin, paprika, Worcestershire sauce and pepper. Trim chicken and cut into 1-inch cubes. Add chicken to marinade and stir to coat; cover and refrigerate for at least 1 hour or up to 4 hours.

Drain chicken; discard marinade. Thread chicken equally on skewers. Rotate the kebobs for 25 to 30 minutes or until cooked through.

Meanwhile, wrap tortillas in foil.and place in the warming tray in the lower position to heat while rotating the skewers.

To eat, place chicken on a tortilla; top with cheese, lettuce and sour cream, roll up and eat with your fingers.

ROTISSERIE &BBQ

Recipe Collection

CHICKEN YAKITORI WITH PEPPERS

Serves 6.

1/2 cup soy sauce
1/4 cup dry sherry
1/4 cup water
1 tablespoon brown sugar
1 teaspoon minced fresh ginger
6 skinless boneless chicken breast halves
6 green onions, white part only
1 red bell pepper, cut into 1-inch squares

Combine the soy sauce, dry sherry, water, brown sugar, and ginger in a small saucepan. Bring to a boil and simmer 1 minute; cool completely.

Cut the chicken into 1-inch cubes and thread on the kebob skewers alternating with the green onions and red pepper cubes. Rotate the kebobs for 25 to 30 minutes or until cooked through.

APRICOT-ORANGE GLAZED GAME HENS

Serves 2 to 4.

1/2 cup apricot preserves
3 tablespoons fresh orange juice
1 tablespoon soy sauce
2 1-1/2 to 2 pound Rock Cornish game hens
Salt and freshly ground pepper

Stir together the preserves, orange juice and soy sauce. Reserve 3 tablespoons of the sauce and place the remaining sauce in the warming tray in the lower position to heat while the hens rotate.

Wash and thoroughly dry the game hens. Season inside cavity with salt and pepper and brush the game hens with the 3 tablespoons of sauce.

Rotate the game hens on the spit rods for 45 to 55 minutes or until the internal temperature reaches 170 degrees on the instant thermometer inserted in the thigh meat. Serve hens with warmed sauce.

CHERRY GLAZED BUTTERFLIED GAME HENS

Serves 2 to 4.

1/2 cup cherry preserves
1/4 cup cranberry or cran-cherry juice
2 tablespoons soy sauce
2 1-1/2 to 2 pound Rock Cornish game hens
Salt and Pepper

Stir together the preserves, juice and soy sauce. Reserve 3 tablespoons of the sauce and place the remaining sauce in the warming tray in the lower position to heat while the hens rotate.

Cut the backbones out of the game hens and flatten by pressing down on the breast bones. Wash and thoroughly dry the game hens. Season both sides with salt and pepper and brush the game hens with the 3 tablespoons of sauce.

Rotate the game hens in the Deep Basket for 40 to 45 minutes or until the internal temperature reaches 170 degrees on the instant thermometer inserted in the thigh meat.   Serve hens with warmed sauce.

BRINE-SOAKED ROAST TURKEY

Serves 10 to 12.

1 cup salt
2 gallons cold water
1 12 to 15 pound turkey
2 tablespoons melted butter

Dissolve the salt in water in a large stock pot or clean bucket. Remove giblets, neck and tail piece from turkey cavity. Rinse turkey thoroughly and place in the brine. Refrigerate turkey in brine for 8 to 12 hours.

Remove turkey from brine and rinse inside and out for several minutes to remove all the salt. Thoroughly pat turkey dry and truss. Brush with melted butter.

Rotate the turkey on the spit rods for 11 to 12 minutes per pound or until the internal temperature reaches 170 degrees on the instant thermometer inserted in the thigh meat. Let the turkey rest for 20 minutes. Carve as usual and serve.

STUFFED TURKEY BREAST WITH CRANBERRY GLAZE

Serves 8.

1 3 to 4 pound boneless turkey half breast
Salt and pepper to taste
1/2 cup dried cranberries
1/4 cup red wine
2 tablespoons unsalted butter
1 medium onion, diced
3 shallots, chopped
3 cloves garlic, minced
3 cups diced French bread
1/2 cup chicken broth
1 egg
1/2 cup toasted pecans
1/2 teaspoon chopped fresh thyme
1/4 teaspoon chopped fresh rosemary
2 tablespoons olive oil
Cranberry Glaze (see page 223)

Butterfly the turkey breast, leaving skin on, by cutting halfway through and opening up. Then pound it slightly with a mallet to even the shape. Season with salt and pepper and set aside.

To make the dressing, soak the dried cranberries in the red wine for 30 minutes or until soft and plump. In a large skillet over medium-high heat, cook the onions, shallots and garlic in the butter for 2 to 3 minutes. Add the plumped cranberries and wine, and cook for 3 to 4 minutes or until all the liquid has evaporated.

In a large bowl toss the bread with the sautéed onion mixture and add enough chicken broth to soften the bread. Add the egg, pecans, thyme, rosemary, and salt and pepper to taste; mix well. Set dressing aside in the refrigerator to cool completely.

Spread the stuffing over the turkey and roll up; tie with kitchen twine. Brush with Cranberry Glaze once before rotating, and again half-way through the rotating. Rotate the turkey roll on the spit rods for 1 hour or until the internal temperature reaches 155 to 160 degrees. Let stand for 10 minutes before carving into generous slices.

TURKEY BURGERS WITH BBQ RUB

Makes 4.

1-1/4 pounds ground turkey
1 tablespoon Dijon mustard
1 tablespoon Worcestershire sauce
1 clove garlic, minced
1/2 teaspoon salt
1/4 teaspoon black pepper
3 tablespoons BBQ Rub (see page 235)

In a medium bowl mix together the turkey, mustard, Worcestershire, garlic, salt and pepper just until combined. Form into 4 patties.

Coat the patties with the rub. Rotate in the Standard Flat Basket for 25 minutes or until cooked through.

ROAST DUCK WITH ORANGE SAUCE

Serves 4.

1/4 cup orange marmalade
1/4 cup fresh orange juice
2 tablespoons soy sauce
1 tablespoon Dijon mustard
1 clove garlic, minced
1 4 to 4-1/2 pound duckling
Salt and pepper

In a small saucepan combine the orange marmalade, orange juice, soy sauce, Dijon and garlic. Bring to a boil and simmer for 5 minutes.

Remove all fat from duck and wash and thoroughly dry both inside and out. Prick duck skin in several places with the tines of a fork. Using an elastic food tie, truss the duck. Season inside and out with salt and pepper.

Rotate on the spit rods for 1-1/2 to 2 hours or until the internal temperature reaches 170 degrees and the juices run clear. Brush the duck with some of the sauce about 15 minutes before the duck is done. Let stand 15 minutes before cutting into serving pieces. Serve with orange sauce.

ROTISSERIE &BBQ
Recipe Collection

PORK

ROTISSERIE
&BBQ

Recipe Collection

PORK LOIN WITH SPICY TEXAS RUB

Serves 6.

SPICY TEXAS RUB:
6 tablespoons paprika
2 tablespoons ground black pepper
2 tablespoons chili powder
2 tablespoons salt
2 tablespoons sugar
1 tablespoon garlic powder
1 tablespoon onion powder
1-1/2 teaspoons cayenne pepper

1 3-1/2 to 4 pound boneless pork loin,
trimmed and tied

To make the rub, mix all the spices together in a bowl. You can store any leftover rub in a tightly sealed jar in the refrigerator for up to 1 month.

Rub a good amount of the spice mixture all over the pork roast to coat completely. Rotate the pork loin on the spit rods for 1 hour 15 to 1 hour 30 minutes or until the internal temperature reaches 160 degrees on the instant thermometer. Remove pork loin, untie and slice into 1/2-inch thick slices to serve.

ITALIAN PORK LOIN
WITH GARLIC AND ROSEMARY

Serves 6.

4 cloves garlic, minced
1/2 teaspoon dried oregano, crumbled
1/2 teaspoon dried rosemary, crumbled
1/4 teaspoon salt
1/4 teaspoon freshly ground pepper
2 tablespoons olive oil
1 3-1/2 to 4 pound boneless pork loin,
trimmed and tied

Stir and mash together the garlic, oregano, rosemary, salt, pepper and olive oil to make a paste. Rub all over the outside of the pork loin, covering as completely as possible.

Rotate the pork roast on the spit rods for 1 hour 15 to 1 hour 30 minutes or until the internal temperature reaches 160 degrees on the instant thermometer. Remove roast, untie and slice into 1/2-inch thick slices to serve.

MARINATED PORK
IN CITRUS HORSERADISH SAUCE

Serves 6.

1 large onion, chopped
6 garlic cloves, crushed
1/2 cup soy sauce
1/4 cup cider vinegar
2 tablespoons vegetable oil
1 tablespoon brown sugar
1 teaspoon curry powder
1 teaspoon oregano
1/2 teaspoon freshly ground pepper
3-1/2 pound boneless pork roast,
trimmed and tied
Citrus Horseradish Sauce (see page 232)

Combine the onion, garlic, soy sauce, vinegar, oil, brown sugar, curry powder, oregano and pepper in a large bowl. Add the pork roast. Cover and marinate 12 to 24 hours, turning occasionally.

Remove the pork from the marinade and rotate the pork roast on the spit rods for 1 hour 15 to 1 hour 30 minutes or until the internal temperature reaches 160 degrees on the instant thermometer. Remove roast, untie and slice into 1/2-inch thick slices. Serve with Citrus Horseradish Sauce.

STUFFED PORK LOIN WITH APPLES

Serves 6.

**2 single pork loins,
(3-1/2 to 4 pounds total)
2 tablespoons unsalted butter
1/2 cup chopped, peeled apple
1/2 cup chopped onion
2 tablespoons dried cherries
1 cup fresh breadcrumbs
1/4 cup minced fresh parsley
1 teaspoon minced fresh rosemary
Salt and pepper
1 egg**

Melt butter in a skillet over medium heat. Add the onion, apple and cherries; sauté until onion is tender. Stir in bread crumbs and cook, stirring often until slightly crisp. Add the parsley, rosemary and salt and pepper. Cool slightly. Add the egg and mix well.

Spread stuffing evenly over one of the pork loins. Top with the other pork loin and tie to hold together. Sprinkle the outside with salt and pepper.

Rotate the pork roast on the spit rods for 1 hour 15 to 1 hour 30 minutes or until the internal temperature reaches 160 degrees on the instant thermometer. Remove roast, untie and slice into 1/2-inch thick slices.

JAMAICAN JERK PORK TENDERLOIN

Serves 4.

**2 tablespoons chopped fresh cilantro
1 tablespoon finely minced fresh ginger
1/4 cup dark rum
2 tablespoons fresh lime juice
2 tablespoons olive oil
2 tablespoons light brown sugar
2 tablespoons soy sauce
1/2 teaspoon nutmeg
1/4 teaspoon cayenne
1/4 teaspoon ground allspice
1/4 teaspoon ground cinnamon
1/4 teaspoon salt
2 pork tenderloins (1-1/2 to 2 pounds total)**

Combine all ingredients except the pork in a flat baking dish. Reserve 1/3 of the marinade and set in the warming tray in the lower position. Trim all fat and silver skin from the pork tenderloins, place in the marinade and turn to coat well. Cover and marinate for 15 to 30 minutes at room temperature. Rotate the pork, one on each spit rod, 30 minutes, basting with the marinating juices often during the last 10 minutes, or until the internal temperature reaches 150 to 155 degrees on the instant thermometer. Slice the pork on the diagonal and place on a serving platter. Spoon reserved marinade over the pork slices and serve.

JALAPENO JELLY GLAZED PORK TENDERLOIN

Serves 4.

Salt and pepper
2 pork tenderloins (1-1/2 to 2 pounds total)
8 tablespoons hot pepper jelly
1/2 cup sour cream

Trim the pork of all fat and silverskin. Generously salt and pepper the tenderloins. Melt 3 tablespoons of the jelly in a small pan over low heat and brush over each tenderloin.

Rotate the pork, one on each spit rod, 30 minutes or until the internal temperature reaches 150 to 155 degrees on the instant thermometer.

While pork is rotating, heat remaining jelly in a small saucepan and stir in the sour cream. Warm slightly, but do not allow to bubble or it will curdle. Slice tenderloins on the diagonal into 1/2-inch medallions, and serve with warm sauce.

BACON WRAPPED PORK TENDERLOIN WITH SAGE

Serves 4.

**2 teaspoons rubbed sage
2 cloves garlic, minced
1/2 teaspoon freshly ground pepper
1/2 teaspoon salt
2 pork tenderloins (1-1/2 to 2 pounds total)
4 slices bacon**

With a mortar and pestle rub the sage, garlic, pepper and salt together. Trim the pork of all fat and silverskin. Rub the sage mixture on the outside of the pork tenderloins. Wrap the pork with the bacon and secure with toothpicks.

Rotate the pork, one on each spit rod, 30 to 35 minutes or until the internal temperature reaches 150 to 155 degrees on the instant thermometer and the bacon is cooked through. Remove bacon and slice pork on a diagonal to serve.

BOURBON SOAKED PORK TENDERLOIN

Serves 4.

1/2 cup soy sauce
1/2 cup Bourbon whiskey
1/4 cup brown sugar
2 pork tenderloins (1-1/2 to 2 pounds total)

Combine soy sauce, Bourbon and brown sugar in a shallow dish. Trim the pork of all fat and silverskin. Add the meat to the marinade, turning to coat. Cover and refrigerate for 3 to 4 hours, turning occasionally.

Rotate the pork, one on each spit rod, 30 to 35 minutes or until the internal temperature reaches 150 to 155 degrees on the instant thermometer. Slice on a diagonal to serve.

CHINESE BBQ PORK TENDERLOIN

Serves 4.

2 cloves garlic, minced
1 tablespoon minced fresh ginger
4 green onions, minced
1/4 cup dry sherry
2 tablespoons soy sauce
3 tablespoons Hoisin sauce
3 tablespoons ketchup
2 tablespoons sugar
1/2 teaspoon salt
1/4 teaspoon freshly ground pepper
2 pork tenderloins (1-1/2 to 2 pounds total)

Combine the garlic, ginger, green onions, sherry, soy sauce, Hoisin sauce, ketchup, sugar, salt and pepper in a shallow dish. Trim the pork of all fat and silverskin. Add the meat to the marinade, turning to coat. Cover and refrigerate for 3 to 4 hours, turning occasionally.

Rotate the pork, one on each spit rod, 30 to 35 minutes or until the internal temperature reaches 150 to 155 degrees on the instant thermometer. Slice on a diagonal to serve.

Recipe Collection

MUSTARD BROWN SUGAR GLAZED PORK CHOPS

Serves 4.

4 1-inch thick center cut pork chops
1/4 cup Dijon mustard
Pinch dried thyme
Pinch dried sage
1/2 cup brown sugar

Wipe pork chops with a paper towel. Stir together mustard, thyme and sage. Coat the pork chops well with the herb mustard. Press brown sugar into the mustard.

Rotate the pork chops in the Flat Standard Basket for 30 to 35 minutes or until cooked through. If not brown enough, position the basket facing the heating coils and push the switch to the pause-to-sear position. Rotate 2 to 3 minutes more on each side.

HERB-CRUSTED PORK CHOPS

Serves 6.

**1 tablespoon dried basil
2 teaspoons dried sage
2 teaspoons garlic powder
2 teaspoons dried thyme
1 teaspoon dried rosemary
1/2 teaspoon dried oregano
6 (3/4-inch thick) boneless pork chops**

Combine basil, sage, garlic powder, thyme, rosemary and oregano in a small bowl or mortar and pestle. Crush to combine well.

Wipe the pork chops with a paper towel and press herb mixture into all the cut surfaces. Rotate immediately or let stand up to one hour at room temperature or refrigerate several hours.

Rotate the pork chops in the Flat Standard Basket for 20 to 25 minutes or until cooked through. If not brown enough, position the basket facing the heating coils and push the switch to the pause-to-sear position. Rotate 2 to 3 minutes on each side.

SPICE RUBBED PORK CHOPS WITH PAPAYA CHUTNEY

Serves 6.

PAPAYA CHUTNEY:
1 large papaya, peeled, seeded and chopped
1 large apple, peeled and chopped
1 cup chopped onion
1/2 red bell pepper, chopped
1/2 cup raisins
3/4 cup sugar
1/2 cup cider vinegar
1/2 teaspoon salt
3/4 teaspoon yellow mustard seeds
1/4 teaspoon crushed red pepper flakes
2 tablespoons crystallized ginger, minced

6 boneless pork loin chops
4 tablespoons Tropical Spice Rub
(see page 237)

Combine chutney ingredients in saucepan and bring to a boil over medium-high heat. Lower heat and simmer until fruit is tender, 30 to 40 minutes. Cool, cover and refrigerate at least 4 hours and up to 2 weeks.

Coat pork chops with the rub and rotate in the Flat Standard Basket for 20 to 25 minutes until cooked through. If not brown enough, position the basket facing the heating coils and push the switch to the pause-to-sear position. Rotate 2 to 3 minutes on each side. Serve with chutney.

STUFFED DRIED FRUIT PORK CHOPS

Serves 4.

1 cup dried apricots, cut up
1/4 cup raisins
1 cup water
2 cups herb stuffing mix
1/4 cup diced celery
2 tablespoons diced onion
1/4 cup butter, melted
Salt and pepper
4 rib pork chops, 1-1/2 inches thick

Combine apricots, raisins and water in a small saucepan. Bring to a simmer; remove from heat and cool.

Drain fruit, reserving liquid, and toss with stuffing mix, celery and onion. Pour melted butter over and stir. Add enough of the reserved fruit liquid to moisten. Season with salt and pepper to taste.

Cut a pocket in the side away from the bone on each chop. Divide stuffing and fill pockets. Rotate the pork chops in the Flat Standard Basket for 35 to 40 minutes or until cooked through. If not brown enough, position the basket facing the heating coils and push the switch to the pause-to-sear position. Rotate 2 to 3 minutes on each side.

PIQUANT PORK KEBOBS

Serves 6.

**1 (12 ounce) jar apricot preserves
1 (8 ounce) bottle Russian salad dressing
1 envelope onion soup mix
1-1/2 pounds boneless pork loin
or tenderloin, cut into 1-inch cubes
1 red bell pepper, cut into 1-inch cubes
2 zucchini, cut into 1-inch pieces**

Combine the preserves, salad dressing and onion soup mix in a bowl. Add the pork cubes, cover and marinate for 4 to 24 hours.

Thread meat alternating with red pepper and zucchini cubes on the kebob skewers. Rotate 25 to 30 minutes or to desired doneness. Remove pork cubes and vegetable cubes to serving plates. Serve with cooked white rice.

BONELESS HAM WITH
BROWN SUGAR PINEAPPLE GLAZE

Serves 6.

1 (16 ounce) can crushed pineapple
1/4 cup brown sugar
1 teaspoon dry mustard
1 4 pound boneless fully cooked ham

In a small saucepan stir together the crushed pineapple, brown sugar and dry mustard. Bring to a simmer and cook for 3 minutes. Set aside to cool.

Insert the spit rods evenly through the ham and brush with some of the pineapple mixture. After 45 minutes of rotating, brush with pineapple mixture again. Rotate an additional 10 or 15 minutes, or until the ham reaches an internal temperature of 140 degrees. Serve sliced ham with some of the pineapple mixture on top.

HAM STEAK
WITH APRICOT-DIJON SAUCE

Serves 2.

2 tablespoons apricot jam
2 tablespoons Dijon mustard
2 tablespoons white wine vinegar
1 clove garlic, minced
Pinch of cayenne pepper
1 ham steak

Stir together the jam, mustard, vinegar, garlic and cayenne. Spread a thin layer over the ham steak.

Rotate the ham steak in the Standard Flat Basket for 15 to 20 minutes or until cooked through. Remove and cut in half to serve.

GROUND PORK PATTIES

Serves 4.

3/4 cup plain dry bread crumbs
1/2 teaspoon ground sage
1/4 teaspoon dried thyme
1/3 cup applesauce
1 egg
2 tablespoons finely chopped green onion
1/2 teaspoon salt
1/4 teaspoon freshly ground pepper
1 pound lean ground pork
4 sesame buns

In a large bowl combine the bread crumbs, sage, thyme, applesauce, egg, green onion, salt and pepper; mix well. Stir in ground pork until well blended. Form into 4 patties, about 3/4 to 1-inch thick.

Rotate in the Standard Flat Basket for 20 to 25 minutes or until cooked through. Remove and serve in the buns with ketchup and lettuce.

ROASTED SAUSAGES WITH PASTA, PEPPERS AND PESTO SAUCE

Serves 4 to 6.

1-1/2 pounds Italian sausages
2 tablespoons olive oil
1 large red bell pepper, slivered
12 ounces button mushrooms, sliced
3/4 cup prepared pesto sauce
Salt and pepper to taste
1 pound linguine, cooked and drained
1/3 cup grated Parmesan cheese

Place the sausages in the Standard Flat Basket and rotate for 15 to 20 minutes or until cooked through. Remove and cut across into 1/2-inch thick slices.

Heat the olive oil in a large skillet and cook the red pepper strips and mushrooms until tender. Add the pesto sauce and sliced sausage. Toss 2 to 3 minutes to warm through. Season to taste with salt and pepper. Toss with linguine and serve with a sprinkling of Parmesan cheese.

ITALIAN SAUSAGE SUB SANDWICH

Serves 4.

8 Italian sausages
4 large French rolls, warmed
1 (16 ounce) jar Spaghetti sauce
8 slices Provolone cheese

Place the sausages in the Standard Flat Basket and rotate for 15 to 20 minutes or until cooked through. Cut sausages in half lengthwise. Place the rolls on the warming tray while the sausages rotate.

Heat Spaghetti sauce in a medium saucepan on top of the stove to a simmer. Add the sausage and simmer for 10 minutes.

When ready to serve, split open the warmed rolls and fill each with 4 sausage slices and 2 slices cheese. Serve immediately.

CHIPOTLE BBQ BABY BACK RIBS

Serves 4.

**4 pounds baby back pork ribs,
cut into 4 pieces
Chipotle BBQ Sauce (see page 220)**

Place ribs in a large pot and cover with water. Bring water to a boil and then simmer for 15 minutes. Remove ribs from water and cool slightly.

Weave ribs on spit rods and baste with Chipotle BBQ sauce. Rotate for 30 minutes or until tender and well browned, basting with sauce one more time. Remove and pour remaining sauce over ribs. Turn to coat and serve.

WHISKEY BASTED ASIAN RIBS

Serves 4.

**4 pounds baby back pork ribs,
cut into 4 pieces
4 large garlic cloves, minced
1 tablespoon minced fresh ginger
1/2 cup soy sauce
1/2 cup Bourbon
1/2 cup Hoisin sauce
1/4 cup honey
3 tablespoons ketchup
3 tablespoons cider vinegar**

Place ribs in a large pot and cover with water. Bring water to a boil and then simmer for 15 minutes. Remove ribs from water.

Combine the garlic, ginger, soy, Bourbon, Hoisin, honey, ketchup, and vinegar in a bowl. Add the ribs and cool to room temperature.

Remove ribs from sauce and weave ribs on spit rods. Rotate for 30 minutes or until tender and well browned, basting with sauce twice during the rotating.

BEEF

Recipe Collection

FOUR PEPPERCORN CRUSTED ROAST BEEF

Serves 4 to 6.

**2 teaspoons black peppercorns
2 teaspoons white peppercorns
2 teaspoons green peppercorns
1 teaspoon pink peppercorns
1 teaspoon salt
1 3-1/2 to 4 pound boneless beef rib roast**

Place the peppercorns in a heavy plastic bag and crush with a rolling pin. Stir in the salt.

Coat the outside of the beef roast with the pepper mixture. Rotate the roast on the spit rods 20 to 25 minutes per pound for rare or until the internal temperature reaches 120 degrees, 30 to 35 minutes per pound for medium, or until the internal temperature reaches 135 degrees, or 40 to 45 minutes per pound for well done, or until the internal temperature reaches 150 degrees on the instant thermometer inserted in the center. Remove and slice in 1/4-inch or thinner slices.

BEEF TENDERLOIN WITH HORSERADISH SAUCE

Serves 6 .

HORSERADISH SAUCE:
3/4 cup whipping cream
4 tablespoons prepared horseradish
2 tablespoons fresh lemon juice
1/2 teaspoon salt

1 3 pound beef tenderloin roast
Salt and pepper

To make the Horseradish Sauce, whip the cream until stiff. Stir in the horseradish, lemon juice and salt. Cover and refrigerate for 1 hour.

Thoroughly coat the beef with salt and pepper. Rotate the beef tenderloin on the spit rods for 30 to 40 minutes or until the internal temperature reaches 125 degrees for rare on the instant thermometer. Remove roast and slice into 1/2-inch thick slices and serve with Horseradish Sauce.

MARINATED TOP SIRLOIN STEAK

Serves 4.

1/2 cup ketchup
2 tablespoons soy sauce
1 tablespoon Worcestershire sauce
1 tablespoon brown sugar
1 clove garlic, minced
1/2 teaspoon chili powder
Salt and pepper to taste
1 1-3/4 to 2 pound sirloin steak

In a flat baking dish stir together the ketchup, soy sauce, Worcestershire sauce, brown sugar, garlic, chili powder, salt and pepper. Add the steak and turn to coat. Cover and marinate in the refrigerator for 2 to 8 hours.

Remove the steak from the marinade. Rotate the steak in the Flat Standard Basket for 15 minutes for rare or 20 minutes for medium. If not brown enough, position the basket facing the heating coils and push the switch to the pause-to-sear position. Rotate 2 to 3 minutes more on each side. Remove and slice thinly across the grain into thin strips.

ROASTED GARLIC STUFFED SIRLOIN

Serves 6 to 8.

1 head roasted garlic (see page 185)
1 tablespoon olive oil
1/2 cup sliced green onions
1 3 pound boneless top sirloin steak
(about 2 inches thick)
Salt and pepper

Squeeze the garlic from the cloves. Mash with the olive oil and stir in the green onions.

Trim any fat from the sirloin and cut a horizontal slit through it to form a pocket the length of the steak. Spread the filling into the pocket. Use toothpicks as needed to secure the stuffing.

Rotate the steak in the Flat Standard Basket for 18 minutes for rare or 22 minutes for medium. If not brown enough, position the basket facing the heating coils and push the switch to the pause-to-sear position. Rotate 2 to 3 minutes more on each side. Remove and slice thinly across the grain into thin strips.

FILET MIGNON
WITH ROASTED GARLIC SAUCE

Serves 4.

**2 whole heads roasted garlic
(see page 185)
1 cup red wine vinegar
3 shallots, finely chopped
2 cups chicken broth
4 1-inch thick beef tenderloin steaks
1 teaspoon crushed black peppercorns**

Combine the wine vinegar and shallots in a small saucepan. Boil until nearly all the liquid has evaporated. Add the chicken broth and boil until reduced to about 1 cup. Squeeze the garlic from the roasted cloves and puree in the food processor or blender. Pour in the broth and puree. Keep warm.

Press the pepper into both sides of the steaks and rotate in the Flat Standard Basket for 15 to 18 minutes or until the meat reaches the desired doneness. Serve topped with roasted garlic.

MUSTARD AND HERB
CRUSTED STEAKS

Serves 2.

1/4 cup Dijon mustard
1 garlic clove, minced
1 green onion, minced
1/2 teaspoon salt
2 1-inch thick rib eye steaks

Combine mustard, garlic, green onion and salt. Spread on both sides of the steaks.

Rotate the steaks in the Flat Standard Basket for 18 minutes for rare or 22 minutes for medium. If not brown enough, position the basket facing the heating coils and push the switch to the pause-to-sear position. Rotate 2 to 3 minutes more on each side.

STEAK WITH SOUTH AMERICAN CHIMICHURRI SAUCE

Serves 4.

1-1/2 pounds steak (top sirloin, Spencer, or rib eye)
Chimichurri Sauce (see page 226)

Rotate the steak in the Flat Standard Basket for 18 minutes for rare or 22 minutes for medium. If not brown enough, position the basket facing the heating coils and push the switch to the pause-to-sear position. Rotate 2 to 3 minutes more on each side. Serve with Chimichurri Sauce on the side.

SPENCER STEAK
WITH BLUE CHEESE SAUCE

Serves 4.

3/4 cup Madeira wine
2 tablespoons minced shallots
1 cup whipping cream
1/2 cup beef broth
1/2 cup unsalted butter
6 ounces Blue cheese, crumbled
2 tablespoons Dijon mustard
Salt and pepper
4 3/4-inch thick Spencer steaks

Mix Madeira and shallots in small saucepan. Boil until reduced to 2 tablespoons. Add cream and beef broth and boil until reduced to 1 cup. Mash butter, blue cheese. Whisk into Madeira mixture a bit at a time. Simmer until creamy. Keep warm.

Rotate the steaks in the Flat Standard Basket for 16 minutes for rare or 20 minutes for medium. If not brown enough, position the basket facing the heating coils and push the switch to the pause-to-sear position. Rotate 2 to 3 minutes more on each side. Serve topped with Blue Cheese Sauce.

STEAK WITH CHILI MUSHROOM SAUCE

Serves 4.

**2 tablespoons olive oil
1 medium onion, chopped
2 (7 ounce) cans chopped green chilies
1 teaspoon minced fresh jalapeno chili
1/4 teaspoon dried oregano
1/4 teaspoon salt
2 tablespoons minced fresh cilantro
4 tablespoons unsalted butter
1/2 pound mushrooms, sliced
1-1/2 pounds steaks (top sirloin,
Spencer, or rib eye)
Spicy Texas Rub (see page 91)**

To make the chili sauce, heat the oil in a small saucepan and add the onion. Cook until soft. Add the chilies, oregano, and salt. Simmer for 5 minutes. Stir in the cilantro. Keep warm.

Heat butter in a small skillet and cook the mushrooms until soft. Keep warm.

Coat the steaks liberally with Spicy Texas Rub and rotate in the Flat Standard Basket for 18 minutes for rare or 22 minutes for medium. If not brown enough, position the basket facing the heating coils and push the switch to the pause-to-sear position. Rotate 2 to 3 minutes more on each side. Top with mushrooms and Chili Sauce.

BBQ BEEF KEBOBS

Serves 6.

**2 pounds beef top sirloin
1 cup prepared BBQ sauce
Cherry tomatoes
Whole mushrooms
Green bell pepper cubes**

Cut the beef into 1-1/2 inch cubes and place in a medium bowl. Stir in BBQ sauce; cover and let marinate for 1 to 4 hours in the refrigerator.

Remove the beef from the sauce and skewer alternating with desired vegetables on the metal skewers.

Rotate the kebobs for 20 to 25 minutes or until rotated to desired doneness, basting with BBQ sauce only during the last 5 minutes of rotating. Remove skewers from the gear wheels and slide the meat and vegetables off onto serving plates.

<u>BEEF FAJITAS</u>

Serves 6.

1 (12 ounce) can beer
2 tablespoons vegetable oil
1/2 medium onion, sliced
Juice of 2 limes
4 cloves garlic, minced
1 bay leaf
2 tablespoons Worcestershire sauce
1 tablespoon chili powder
1 teaspoon ground cumin
1 teaspoon freshly ground pepper
1-1/2 pounds top sirloin steak
6 flour tortillas, warmed
Purchased salsa

In a large flat dish combine the beer, oil, onion, lime juice, garlic, bay leaf, Worcestershire, chili powder, cumin and pepper. Stir well. Add the steak, cover and refrigerate 24 hours.

Rotate the steak in the Flat Standard Basket for 18 minutes for rare or 22 minutes for medium. If not brown enough, position the basket facing the heating coils and push the switch to the pause-to-sear position. Rotate 2 to 3 minutes more on each side. Place the tortillas in the warming tray while rotating the steak.

Slice the steak into thin strips. Fill tortillas with steak strips and salsa. Roll up and serve.

BLUE CHEESE STUFFED HAMBURGERS

Serves 4.

**1-1/2 pounds lean ground beef
4 ounces blue cheese
2 tablespoons minced green onions
Salt and pepper**

Divide ground beef and form into 8 patties. Mash together the blue cheese and green onions. Divide evenly into quarters and place on 4 of the patties. Top with remaining 4 patties and press to seal the edges. Season the outside well with salt and pepper.

Rotate in the Flat Standard Basket for 20 minutes for medium well or until cooked to desired doneness. If not brown enough, position the basket facing the heating coils and push the switch to the pause-to-sear position. Rotate 2 to 3 minutes more on each side.

MUSHROOM STUFFED BURGERS

Serves 4.

**2 tablespoons butter
1/2 pound button mushrooms, thinly sliced
2 tablespoons minced green onions
1 clove garlic, minced
Salt and pepper
1-1/2 pounds lean ground beef**

Melt the butter in a medium skillet over medium-high heat. Add the mushrooms, green onions and garlic and cook until mushrooms are lightly browned. Season to taste with salt and pepper. Set aside to cool to room temperature.

Divide ground beef and form into 8 patties. Divide the mushroom mixture evenly into quarters and place on 4 of the patties. Top with remaining 4 patties and press to seal the edges. Season the outside well with salt and pepper.

Rotate in the Flat Standard Basket for 20 minutes for medium-well or until cooked to desired doneness. If not brown enough, position the basket facing the heating coils and push the switch to the pause-to-sear position. Rotate 2 to 3 minutes more on each side.

WINE AND HONEY MARINATED SHORT RIBS

Serves 4 to 6.

1 (8 ounce) can tomato sauce
1/2 cup dry red wine
1/4 cup honey
1/2 cup red wine vinegar
1 small onion, chopped
2 cloves garlic, minced
1/8 teaspoon ground cloves
4 pounds beef short ribs

In a shallow baking dish combine the tomato sauce, red wine, honey, vinegar, onion, garlic and cloves. Stir well. Add the short ribs and turn to coat with the sauce. Cover and refrigerate for 24 hours.

Remove the ribs from the sauce. Transfer sauce to a small saucepan and set on the stove. Rotate ribs in the Deep Basket for 1 hour, basting the ribs every 15 minutes until cooked through and well browned.

Bring the reserved sauce to a boil and then simmer for 5 minutes. Serve sauce with the short ribs.

Recipe Collection

LAMB

ROTISSERIE & BBQ

Recipe Collection

MERLOT MARINATED LEG OF LAMB

Serves 6 to 8.

1/2 cup soy sauce
1 cup Merlot or other dry red wine
4 cloves garlic, minced
2 tablespoons dried oregano
1 tablespoon dried rosemary
1 tablespoon coarsely ground pepper
1 leg of lamb (4-1/2 to 5 pounds),
boned and tied

Combine soy sauce, Merlot, garlic, oregano, rosemary and pepper in a deep bowl. Add lamb and turn to coat with marinade. Cover and chill at least 6 hours or up to 1 day, turning meat over several times. Remove lamb from marinade, reserving marinade for basting.

Rotate the lamb on the spit rods for 1 hour 15 to 1 hour 30 minutes or until the internal temperature reaches 135 to 140 degrees for medium on the instant thermometer, basting several times during the last 10 minutes. Untie, slice and serve.

DIJON-GARLIC-ROSEMARY RUBBED LAMB ROAST

Serves 6 to 8.

1 clove garlic, cut into slivers
1/2 cup Dijon mustard
2 tablespoons soy sauce
2 teaspoons chopped fresh rosemary
1/2 teaspoon ground ginger
2 tablespoons olive oil
1 leg of lamb (4-1/2 to 5 pounds),
boned and tied

Combine the garlic, Dijon mustard, soy sauce, rosemary, ginger and olive oil in a small bowl. Add lamb and turn to coat with marinade. Cover and chill at least 6 hours or up to 1 day turning meat over several times.

Rotate the lamb on the spit rods for 1 hour 15 to 1 hour 30 minutes or until the internal temperature reaches 135 to 140 degrees for medium on the instant thermometer, basting several times during the last 10 minutes. Untie, slice and serve.

MINTY LAMB CHOPS
WITH HERB BUTTER

Serves 4.

**1/3 cup chopped fresh mint
1 clove garlic, minced
Juice of 1 lemon
1/2 cup olive oil
Salt and pepper
8 loin lamb chops**

**HERB BUTTER:
1/2 cup butter, at room temperature
2 tablespoons minced fresh mint
1 tablespoon minced fresh parsley
2 cloves garlic, minced**

Combine mint, garlic, lemon juice and olive oil in food processor or blender. Season with salt and pepper. Pour over the lamb chops, cover and refrigerate at least 4 hours.

Mash together the Herb Butter ingredients, form into a log shape, wrap in plastic wrap and refrigerate.

Rotate chops in the Standard Flat Basket for 15 minutes for medium rare. If not brown enough, position the basket facing the heating coils and push the switch to the pause-to-sear position. Rotate 2 to 3 minutes more on each side. Serve topped with a 1/2-inch slice of the Herb Butter.

LAMB CHOPS WITH MINTED HORSERADISH SAUCE

Serves 4.

MINTED HORSERADISH SAUCE:
1/2 cup sour cream
2 teaspoons prepared horseradish
1 tablespoon chopped fresh mint

2 tablespoons Dijon mustard
2 cloves garlic, minced
8 loin lamb chops

To make the Minted Horseradish Sauce, combine the sour cream, horseradish, and mint in a small bowl. Cover and refrigerate at least 2 hours and up to 24 hours.

Stir the garlic into the mustard and spread on both sides of the chops. Rotate in the Flat Standard Basket for 15 minutes for medium-rare. If not brown enough, position the basket facing the heating coils and push the switch to the pause-to-sear position. Rotate 2 to 3 minutes more on each side. Serve chops topped with a dollop of the Minted Horseradish Sauce.

LAMB KEBOBS WITH
BLACKBERRY-MUSTARD GLAZE

Serves 6.

**2 pounds boneless leg of lamb,
cut into 1-inch cubes
1/3 cup olive oil
1/4 cup tarragon vinegar
2 tablespoons soy sauce
1 clove garlic, minced
1 tablespoon minced fresh rosemary
1/2 teaspoon salt
1/2 cup seedless blackberry jam
1/4 cup Dijon mustard**

In a large bowl combine the olive oil, vinegar, soy sauce, garlic, rosemary and salt. Add the lamb cubes. Toss well to coat and cover and refrigerate overnight.

Thread lamb onto kebob skewers. Rotate for 20 minutes or until cooked to desired doneness.

Combine jam and mustard in a small saucepan over medium heat on the stove to dissolve the jam. Brush over the kebobs and serve.

MUSTARD SHISH KEBOBS

Serves 4.

**2 pounds boneless leg of lamb,
cut into 1-inch cubes
3 tablespoons Dijon mustard
2 tablespoons white wine vinegar
2 tablespoons olive oil
1 teaspoon minced fresh rosemary
or 1/4 teaspoon dried rosemary
1/4 teaspoon dried sage
2 cloves garlic, minced
Salt and pepper
1 green bell pepper cut into 1-inch squares
1 red bell pepper, cut into 1-inch squares**

Combine the mustard, vinegar, olive oil, rosemary, sage, garlic, salt and pepper in a bowl. Add the lamb and toss to coat thoroughly. Cover and refrigerate for 24 hours.

Thread lamb onto kebob skewers alternating with pepper squares. Rotate for 20 minutes or until cooked to desired doneness.

LAMB

139

ROTISSERIE &BBQ

Recipe Collection

Recipe Collection

SEAFOOD

ROTISSERIE &BBQ

Recipe Collection

LEMON-DILL SALMON STEAKS

Serves 4.

**1/3 cup fresh lemon juice
2 tablespoons olive oil
1 tablespoon minced fresh dill or
1 teaspoon dried dill weed
1/2 teaspoon salt
1/4 teaspoon white pepper
4 medium salmon steaks**

In a flat baking dish or food storage bag combine the lemon juice, olive oil, dill, salt and pepper. Add the salmon and turn to coat all sides. Cover or seal tightly and marinate in the refrigerator for 20 minutes to 2 hours.

Rotate the salmon in the Flat Standard Basket for 15 to 20 minutes or until just cooked through.

BROWN SUGAR CURED SALMON FILLETS

Serves 4 to 6.

2 tablespoons light brown sugar
2 tablespoons cider vinegar
2 teaspoons coarse salt
1/2 teaspoon freshly ground pepper
1-1/2 pounds salmon fillets, with skin

Cut salmon on flesh side in a crisscross pattern. Combine the brown sugar, vinegar, salt and pepper and brush or spoon on the fleshy side of the fish. Wrap in plastic wrap and then place in a tightly sealed plastic bag. Refrigerate up to 24 hours.

Rotate the salmon in the Flat Standard Basket for 12 to 18 minutes or until just cooked through. Cut into serving size pieces and serve.

SALMON WITH CUCUMBER SAUCE

Serves 4.

**1-1/2 pounds salmon fillets,
cut into serving pieces
Juice of 1 lemon**

**CUCUMBER SAUCE:
1 medium cucumber
1/2 teaspoon salt
1-1/2 teaspoons white vinegar
1 small clove garlic, minced
1 tablespoon snipped fresh dill
1 cup plain yogurt
2 teaspoons olive oil**

Drizzle the lemon juice over the salmon and rotate the salmon in the Flat Standard Basket for 10 to 15 minutes or until just cooked through. Serve with Cucumber Sauce.

To make the Cucumber Sauce, peel the cucumber and halve lengthwise. Remove the seeds from the center of the cucumbers, then grate. Place in a bowl and sprinkle with salt. Refrigerate for 1 hour. In another bowl, stir together the vinegar, garlic, dill, yogurt, and olive oil. Drain the cucumbers and add to the yogurt mixture. Refrigerate for at least 4 hours before serving.

SALMON WITH BASIL PESTO RUB

Serves 4.

**4 salmon steaks
Juice of 1 lemon
Basil Pesto Rub (see page 240)**

Drizzle the lemon juice over the salmon and brush with Basil Pesto Rub. Rotate the salmon in the Flat Standard Basket for 12 to 18 minutes or until just cooked through. Serve with a dollop of Pesto sauce.

CAJUN BLACKENED RED SNAPPER

Serves 4.

**1-1/2 pounds red snapper, cut into serving-size pieces
2 tablespoons melted butter
Cajun-Creole Rub (see page 236)**

Brush the fish with butter and dredge in the Cajun-Creole Rub to coat well.

Rotate the fish in the Flat Standard Basket for 15 to 20 minutes or until just cooked through.

SNAPPER FILLETS WITH TOMATO-CILANTRO SAUCE

Serves 4.

**1-1/2 pounds red snapper, cut into serving-size pieces
1 tablespoon olive oil**

**TOMATO-CILANTRO SAUCE:
1 tablespoon olive oil
1 medium onion, thinly sliced
3 cloves garlic, minced
2 cups peeled, diced fresh tomatoes
1 serrano chili, minced
2 tablespoons minced fresh cilantro
1 teaspoon ground coriander
1 teaspoon ground cumin
1 bay leaf
Salt and freshly ground pepper to taste**

Brush fish with olive oil. Rotate the fish in the Flat Standard Basket for 15 to 20 minutes or until just cooked through.

For the sauce, heat the oil in a saucepan over medium-high heat. Add onion and garlic until softened. Add the tomatoes, serrano chili, fresh cilantro, coriander, cumin, and bay leaf. Bring to a boil; reduce heat and simmer, uncovered, 10 minutes. Season to taste with salt and pepper. Pour over cooked fish to serve.

HALIBUT WITH MUSTARD DILL SAUCE

Serves 4.

**1-1/2 to 2 pounds halibut steaks
1 tablespoon olive oil
Mustard Dill Sauce (see page 229)**

Brush fish with olive oil. Rotate the fish in the Flat Standard Basket for 15 to 20 minutes or until just cooked through. Serve with Mustard Dill Sauce.

ORANGE FLAVORED TUNA

Serves 4.

1/2 cup unsalted butter
1 tablespoon dry vermouth
1 tablespoon orange juice
1 tablespoon grated orange zest
2 cloves garlic, minced
1 teaspoon steak sauce
1 teaspoon Cajun-Creole Rub
(see page 236)
1/4 teaspoon hot pepper sauce
4 tuna steaks

Place the butter, vermouth, orange juice and zest, garlic, steak sauce, Cajun-Creole Rub, and hot pepper sauce in a saucepan and heat until butter melts, mixture boils and ingredients are well blended, stirring frequently.

Brush the tuna steaks with some of the sauce and rotate in the Flat Standard Basket for 15 to 20 minutes or until barely cooked through. Serve with the remaining warmed sauce poured over the fish.

TERIYAKI TUNA OR SWORDFISH

Serves 4.

Teriyaki Ginger Marinade (see page 215)
4 tuna or swordfish steaks
2 tablespoons minced green onions

Prepare the marinade and pour over the fish. Cover and refrigerate for 1 hour. Rotate the fish in the Flat Standard Basket for 15 to 20 minutes or until just cooked through. Sprinkle with green onions and serve.

CURRIED SWORDFISH STEAKS

Serves 4.

1/3 cup olive oil
3 tablespoons fresh lime juice
2 tablespoons soy sauce
1 tablespoon honey
1 teaspoon minced garlic
1 teaspoon minced ginger
1/2 cup chopped fresh cilantro
1 teaspoon curry powder
1/2 teaspoon salt
1/4 teaspoon freshly ground pepper
4 swordfish steaks

Combine the olive oil, lime juice, soy, honey, garlic, ginger, cilantro, curry powder, salt and pepper in the blender or food processor and puree until smooth. Pour over the swordfish, cover and refrigerate at least 30 minutes and up to 2 hours.

Rotate the fish in the Flat Standard Basket for 15 to 20 minutes or until just cooked through.

STUFFED SOLE FILLETS
WITH MARINARA SAUCE

Serves 6.

2 cups prepared Marinara Sauce
2 pounds large sole fillets
Salt and pepper
1 cup fine dry breadcrumbs
2 tablespoons minced fresh parsley
1/4 cup freshly grated Parmesan cheese
1/4 cup chopped black olives
2 tablespoons capers
2 tablespoons olive oil

Heat Marinara Sauce in a small saucepan over medium heat. Keep warm.

Lay the fish fillets out on a work surface. Sprinkle with salt and pepper. Toss together the breadcrumbs, parsley, Parmesan cheese, olives and capers. Divide and distribute over the top of the fish fillets. Roll up and secure with toothpicks.

Brush fish with olive oil. Rotate the fish rolls in the Flat Standard Basket for 15 to 20 minutes or until just cooked through. Serve topped with hot Marinara Sauce.

SWEET-SOUR SHRIMP BROCHETTES

Serves 4.

SWEET AND SOUR SAUCE:
2 tablespoons cornstarch
1 cup pineapple juice
2 tablespoons cider vinegar
1/2 cup brown sugar
1 tablespoon ketchup
1 tablespoon soy sauce

1 pound extra-large shrimp,
peeled and deveined
1 red or yellow bell pepper,
cut into 1-inch cubes

To make the Sweet and Sour Sauce, stir the cornstarch into the pineapple juice in a small saucepan. Stir in the vinegar, brown sugar, ketchup and soy sauce. Cook over medium heat, until the sauce boils, thickens and clears, stirring often. Remove 1/2 cup and set in the warming tray in the upper warming position.

Skewer the shrimp, alternating with the bell pepper cubes on the metal skewers. Rotate the kebobs for 15 minutes or until shrimp turn bright orange in color. Remove skewers from the gear wheels and slide the shrimp and peppers off onto serving plates. Serve with warm Sweet and Sour Sauce.

SKEWERED SHRIMP AND SCALLOPS WITH SAGE-LEMON BUTTER

Serves 6.

3 tablespoons olive oil
Grated zest of 1/2 lemon
2 cloves garlic
18 extra large shrimp, shelled and deveined
18 large sea scallops
2 tablespoons minced fresh parsley

SAGE-LEMON BUTTER:
1/2 cup butter
1 tablespoon fresh lemon juice
1 teaspoon dried sage leaves
Grated zest of 1/2 lemon

Stir together the olive oil, lemon zest and garlic. Skewer the scallops and shrimp alternately on six kebob skewers. Brush with the olive oil mixture. Rotate the kebobs for 15 minutes or until the shrimp turn pink.

To make Sage-Lemon Butter, melt butter in a small saucepan. Whisk in lemon juice, sage and lemon zest. Set aside.

Transfer shellfish to a serving dish and pour Sage-Lemon Butter over. Garnish with parsley.

SCALLOP KEBOBS WITH BACON AND WATER CHESTNUTS

Serves 4.

12 strips thinly sliced bacon
16 large sea scallops
16 small water chestnuts
1/3 cup soy sauce
2 tablespoons rice vinegar
1-1/2 tablespoons sugar
1 tablespoon dry sherry
1 garlic clove, minced
1 teaspoon minced fresh ginger

Partially rotate the bacon until light brown and cut into pieces the same size as the scallops. Thread the bacon, scallops and water chestnuts alternately on 8 kebob skewers.

In a shallow dish, stir together the soy sauce, rice vinegar, sugar, sherry, garlic and ginger. Add the skewers and turn to coat in the marinade. Cover and refrigerate for 2 to 3 hours, turning occasionally.

Rotate the kebobs for 15 minutes or until the scallops are firm and cooked through and the bacon is crisp.

LOBSTER TAILS WITH GARLIC BUTTER

Serves 4.

**8 frozen lobster tails, thawed
1/2 cup unsalted butter
2 tablespoons fresh lemon juice
4 cloves garlic, minced**

Cut the lobster tails lengthwise through shell, then open flat. In a small saucepan, melt the butter with lemon juice and garlic. Brush some on the lobster. Rotate the lobster in the Flat Standard Basket for 15 to 20 minutes or until firm and opaque. Serve with remaining butter for dipping.

ROTISSERIE WRAPS

ROTISSERIE
&BBQ

Recipe Collection

LEMON CHICKEN WITH ZUCCHINI AND RED PEPPERS

Serves 4.

4 boneless skinless chicken breast halves
Lemon-Garlic Marinade (see page 209)
1 medium zucchini, diced
1 small red bell pepper, diced
2 (14 x 12 inch) sheets heavy-duty
aluminum foil

Wash and pat dry the chicken breasts. Make the marinade and immerse the chicken. Cover and refrigerate 30 to 60 minutes.

Lay the chicken breasts on one sheet of foil. Top with the zucchini and peppers and drizzle with 2 tablespoons marinade. Top with second sheet of foil and fold the edges over three times to seal the foil packet. Rotate in the Flat Standard Basket for 20 minutes.

SOUTHWESTERN CHICKEN
WITH CORN AND PEPPERS

Serves 4.

4 skinless chicken breast halves
Southwestern Rub (see page 237)
2 tablespoons butter
1/4 cup diced red bell pepper
1/4 cup diced green bell pepper
1 cup frozen corn, thawed
2 (14 x 12 inch) sheets heavy-duty
aluminum foil

Wash and pat dry the chicken breasts. Coat well with the rub and place on one sheet of foil.

Sauté the peppers and corn in the butter in a small skillet. Spoon over the chicken. Top with second sheet of foil and fold the edges over three times to seal the foil packet.

Rotate in the Flat Standard Basket for 30 minutes or until cooked through.

BOURBON ORANGE
BBQ CHICKEN THIGHS

Serves 4 to 6.

6 skinless chicken thighs
1 cup Bourbon-Orange BBQ Sauce
(see page 221)
2 (14 x 12 inch) sheets heavy-duty
aluminum foil

Wash and pat dry the chicken thighs. Place on one sheet of foil. Spoon on BBQ sauce. Top with second sheet of foil and fold the edges over three times to seal the foil packet.

Rotate in the Flat Standard Basket for 30 to 35 minutes or until cooked through.

CHINESE BBQ CHICKEN

Serves 4.

**4 boneless skinless chicken breast halves
Hoisin BBQ Sauce (see page 222)
2 tablespoons minced fresh cilantro
2 (14 x 12 inch) sheets heavy-duty
aluminum foil**

Wash and pat dry the chicken breasts. Place on one sheet of foil. Spoon on the sauce and sprinkle with cilantro. Top with second sheet of foil and fold the edges over three times to seal the foil packet. Rotate in the Flat Standard Basket for 20 minutes.

CHICKEN CACCIATORE

Serves 4.

**4 boneless skinless chicken breast halves
1 cup prepared Marinara Sauce
8 mushrooms, quartered
1/4 cup diced green bell pepper
2 (14 x 12 inch) sheets heavy-duty
aluminum foil**

Wash and pat dry the chicken breasts. Place chicken on one sheet of foil. Top with Marinara sauce, mushrooms and bell pepper. Top with second sheet of foil and fold the edges over three times to seal the foil packet. Rotate in the Flat Standard Basket for 20 minutes.

GARLIC ORANGE CHICKEN

Serves 4.

**4 boneless skinless chicken breast halves
2 cloves garlic, minced
1/4 cup olive oil
1 teaspoon grated orange zest
1/4 teaspoon dry rosemary leaves
2 slices orange
2 (14 x 12 inch) sheets heavy-duty
aluminum foil**

Wash and pat dry the chicken. Lay in a flat baking dish. Combine the garlic, olive oil, orange zest and rosemary in a small bowl. Pour over the chicken and marinate for 2 hours in the refrigerator.

Lay chicken on one sheet of foil. Top with the orange slices and 2 tablespoons of the marinade. Top with second sheet of foil and fold the edges over three times to seal the foil packet. Rotate in the Flat Standard Basket for 20 minutes.

RASPBERRY CHICKEN

Serves 4.

4 boneless skinless chicken breast halves
Raspberry Marinade (see page 210)
2 tablespoons minced chives
2 (14 x 12 inch) sheets heavy-duty
aluminum foil

Wash and pat dry the chicken breasts. Marinate in the Raspberry Marinade for 2 hours, covered in the refrigerator.

Place chicken on one sheet of foil. Sprinkle with chives. Top with second sheet of foil and fold the edges over three times to seal the foil packet. Rotate in the Flat Standard Basket for 20 minutes.

CUMBERLAND TURKEY SLICES

Serves 2 to 4.

4 slices turkey breast
1/2 cup Cumberland Sauce (see page 224)
1 tablespoon minced green onions
2 (14 x 12 inch) sheets heavy-duty
aluminum foil

Lay turkey slices on one sheet of foil. Top with Cumberland Sauce and sprinkle with green onions. Top with second sheet of foil and fold the edges over three times to seal the foil packet. Rotate in the Flat Standard Basket for 15 to 20 minutes.

CURRY SHRIMP WITH SNOW PEAS

Serves 4.

1 pound raw shrimp, cleaned and deveined
Thai Red Curry Sauce (see page 227)
8 fresh snow peas, cut in thin strips
2 (14 x 12 inch) sheets heavy-duty
aluminum foil

Place shrimp on one sheet of foil. Top with sauce and then snow peas. Top with second sheet of foil and fold the edges over three times to seal the foil packet. Rotate in the Flat Standard Basket for 15 minutes.

167

SPICY PEPPER SHRIMP

Serves 4.

1 pound raw shrimp, cleaned and deveined
Lime-Chili Marinade (see page 212)
1/4 cup diced red bell pepper
2 tablespoons diced Anaheim chili
2 (14 x 12 inch) sheets heavy-duty
aluminum foil

Combine the shrimp and marinade in a bowl. Cover and refrigerate for 30 minutes.

Place shrimp on one sheet of foil. Top with red pepper and chili. Top with second sheet of foil and fold the edges over three times to seal the foil packet. Rotate in the Flat Standard Basket for 15 minutes.

SEA BASS WITH FRESH TOMATOES

Serves 4.

**4 small sea bass fillets
2 plum tomatoes, seeded and diced
2 tablespoons minced green onions
2 tablespoons butter
Salt and pepper
2 (14 x 12 inch) sheets heavy-duty
aluminum foil**

Place fish on one sheet of foil. Top with tomatoes and green onions. Dot with butter and sprinkle with salt and pepper. Top with second sheet of foil and fold edges over three times to seal the foil packet. Rotate in the Flat Standard Basket for 15 minutes.

TROPICAL SPICED SALMON STEAKS

Serves 2.

**2 salmon steaks
Tropical Sweet Spice Rub (see page 237)
2 tablespoons butter
4 (8 x 6 inch) sheets heavy-duty
aluminum foil**

Coat salmon with Spice Rub. Place each salmon steak on one sheet of foil. Dot with butter. Top with second sheet of foil and fold edges over three times to seal the foil packet. Rotate in the Flat Standard Basket for 15 minutes.

MEDITERRANEAN SNAPPER

Serves 2.

2 red snapper fillets
2 tablespoons olive oil
1 tablespoon balsamic vinegar
2 plum tomatoes, seeded and diced
1 tablespoon capers, rinsed
2 tablespoons minced Kalamata olives
Pinch dried red pepper flakes
1 tablespoon minced fresh basil leaves
2 tablespoons butter
Salt and pepper
2 (14 x 12 inch) sheets heavy-duty
aluminum foil

Place fish on one sheet of foil. In a small bowl toss together the olive oil, vinegar, tomatoes, capers, olives, red pepper flakes and basil. Spoon over the fish. Dot with butter and sprinkle with salt and pepper. Top with second sheet of foil and fold edges over three times to seal the foil packet. Rotate in the Flat Standard Basket for 15 minutes.

SOLE AND SHRIMP
IN BUTTER-WINE SAUCE

Serves 4.

4 large pieces fillet of sole
1 cup small cooked shrimp
2 tablespoons minced green onions
2 tablespoons butter
1/2 cup dry white wine
Salt and pepper to taste
2 (14 x 12 inch) sheets heavy-duty
aluminum foil

Lay the fish on a work surface. Toss shrimp with green onions and spread over the fish. Roll fish up and place on one sheet of the foil. In a small saucepan, melt the butter and add the wine. Spoon the wine over the fish fillets. Top with second sheet of foil and fold edges over three times to seal the foil packet. Rotate in the Flat Standard Basket for 15 minutes.

GINGERED HAM AND PINEAPPLE

Serves 2 to 3.

**1 ham steak
1 (8 ounce) can pineapple slices
1/4 cup pineapple juice from can
2 tablespoons brown sugar
1/2 teaspoon ground ginger
2 (14 x 12 inch) sheets heavy-duty
aluminum foil**

Lay the ham on one sheet of the foil. Lay the pineapple on the ham. Stir the brown sugar and ginger into the pineapple juice and spoon over the ham. Top with second sheet of foil and fold edges over three times to seal the foil packet. Rotate in the Flat Standard Basket for 10 minutes.

CRANBERRY SAUCE

Makes 1-1/2 cups.

**1 (12 ounce) bag fresh cranberries
1 cup sugar
1/4 cup fresh orange juice
2 (14 x 12 inch) sheets heavy-duty
aluminum foil**

Toss together cranberries, sugar and orange juice. Place on one sheet of foil. Top with second sheet of foil and fold edges over three times to seal the foil packet. Rotate in the Flat Standard Basket for 15 minutes.

TROPICAL PORK MEDALLIONS

Serves 2 to 3.

**1 pork tenderloin
Tropical Rum Lime Marinade (see page 211)
2 tablespoons minced fresh cilantro
2 (14 x 12 inch) sheets heavy-duty
aluminum foil**

Trim all fat and silverskin from the pork and slice into 1-inch thick medallions. Prepare the marinade and add the pork slices. Cover and refrigerate for 1 hour.

Remove pork from marinade and place on one sheet of the foil. Sprinkle with cilantro. Top with second sheet of foil and fold edges over three times to seal the foil packet. Rotate in the Flat Standard Basket for 15 minutes.

ROASTED ZUCCHINI WITH RED ONION

Serves 4.

4 small zucchini, cut lengthwise
1 small red onion, sliced
2 tablespoons olive oil
Salt and pepper
2 tablespoons chopped parsley
2 (14 x 12 inch) sheets heavy-duty
aluminum foil

Lay zucchini cut side up on one sheet of foil. Top with onion; drizzle with oil and sprinkle with salt, pepper and parsley. Top with second sheet of foil and fold edges over three times to seal the foil packet. Rotate in the Flat Standard Basket for 15 minutes.

BAKED SWEET POTATOES AND APPLES

Serves 4.

2 medium sweet potatoes,
peeled and sliced
2 medium apples, peeled and sliced
1/4 cup brown sugar
2 tablespoons butter, melted
2 (14 x 12 inch) sheets heavy-duty
aluminum foil

Lay the sweet potato and apple slices on one sheet of foil. Sprinkle with brown sugar and drizzle with butter. Top with second sheet of foil and fold edges over three times to seal the foil packet. Rotate in the Flat Standard Basket for 30 minutes.

ROASTED GINGER
AND ORANGE CARROTS

Serves 4.

**1 pound carrots, peeled and halved
crosswise and lengthwise
3 tablespoons butter, melted
1 tablespoon minced fresh ginger
2 tablespoons fresh orange juice
1 teaspoon grated orange zest
1 tablespoon honey
Salt and pepper
1 tablespoon minced fresh parsley
2 (14 x 12 inch) sheets heavy-duty
aluminum foil**

Lay carrots on one sheet of foil. Toss together the butter, ginger, orange juice and zest and honey. Drizzle over the carrots. Sprinkle with salt, pepper and parsley. Top with second sheet of foil and fold edges over three times to seal the foil packet. Rotate in the Flat Standard Basket for 20 minutes.

ITALIAN ZUCCHINI, MUSHROOMS AND PEPPERS

Serves 4.

**4 small zucchini,
cut into 1/2-inch thick slices
8 large mushrooms
1/2 red bell pepper, diced
2 tablespoons olive oil
1/2 teaspoon Italian herb seasoning
Salt and pepper
2 (14 x 12 inch) inch sheets heavy-duty
aluminum foil**

Place zucchini, mushrooms and bell pepper on one sheet of foil. Drizzle with olive oil, Italian herb seasoning, salt and pepper. Top with second sheet of foil and fold edges over three times to seal the foil packet. Rotate in the Flat Standard Basket for 15 minutes.

CURRIED FRUIT

Serves 4.

**1 (16 ounce) can sliced peaches, drained
1 (16 ounce) can pear halves,
drained & quartered
10 maraschino cherries
1 (8 ounce) can pineapple chunks
(reserve 2 tablespoons juice)
2 tablespoons butter
1/4 cup brown sugar
2 teaspoons curry powder
2 (14 x 12 inch) sheets heavy-duty
aluminum foil**

Arrange fruit on one sheet of foil. Stir together the pineapple juice, butter, brown sugar and curry powder. Drizzle over the fruit. Top with second sheet of foil and fold edges over three times to seal the foil packet. Rotate in the Flat Standard Basket for 10 minutes.

BAKED APPLES AND DRIED
CRANBERRIES WITH MAPLE BUTTER

Serves 4.

**3 medium apples, peeled and sliced
1/2 cup dried cranberries
2 tablespoons butter, melted
1/4 cup real maple syrup
1/2 teaspoon ground cinnamon
2 (14 x 12 inch) sheets heavy-duty
aluminum foil**

Place the apples and dried cranberries on one sheet of foil. Stir together the butter, maple syrup and cinnamon. Drizzle over the fruit. Top with second sheet of foil and fold edges over three times to seal the foil packet. Rotate in the Flat Standard Basket for 25 minutes.

SPICED PEARS OVER ICE CREAM

Serves 4.

4 medium-ripe pears, peeled and cubed
1/2 teaspoon cinnamon
1/8 teaspoon ground cloves
Dash ground cardamom
1/3 cup brown sugar
2 tablespoons butter, melted
Vanilla ice cream
2 (14 x 12 inch) sheets heavy-duty
aluminum foil

Toss pears with spices and brown sugar. Place on one sheet of the foil. Drizzle with butter. Top with second sheet of foil and fold edges over three times to seal the foil packet. Rotate in the Flat Standard Basket for 20 minutes. Serve over Vanilla ice cream.

ROTISSERIE & BBQ

Recipe Collection

VEGETABLES

ROTISSERIE
&BBQ

Recipe Collection

ROASTED VEGETABLE SKEWERS WITH BASIL MARINADE

Serves 6.

1 red bell pepper, cut into 1-inch pieces
1 yellow summer squash,
cut into 1/4-inch slices
1 zucchini, cut into 1/4-inch slices
16 cherry tomatoes
16 white button mushrooms,
stems removed
8 green onions, cut into 1-1/2 inch pieces

MARINADE:
1/2 cup olive oil
6 tablespoons balsamic vinegar
2 tablespoons minced fresh basil
2 cloves garlic, minced
Salt and pepper to taste

Prepare vegetables and place in a large bowl or food storage bag. Combine marinade ingredients and pour over vegetables. Cover and marinate 1 to 2 hours at room temperature.

Drain off marinade and skewer vegetables on Kebob Rods. Rotate the skewered vegetables for 20 to 25 minutes or until vegetables are cooked through but still crunchy. Remove skewers from the gear wheels and slide the vegetables off onto serving plates.

MIXED VEGETABLES
WITH ITALIAN HERBS

Serves 4 to 6.

1 zucchini, cut into 1-inch cubes
1 yellow crookneck squash,
cut into 1-inch cubes
1 red bell pepper, cut into 1-inch squares
1/2 pound button mushrooms,
stems trimmed
1 onion, cut into wedges
2 tablespoons olive oil
1 teaspoon mixed Italian herbs
Salt and pepper

In a large bowl, toss together all the vegetables.
Add the olive oil, Italian herbs, salt and pepper.
Toss well. Rotate in the Deep Basket for 25 to
30 minutes or until crispy and tender.

ROASTED GARLIC

Makes 4 roasted heads.

4 heads garlic
4 tablespoons olive oil

Cut the tops of the garlic off, exposing the cloves. Set each head of garlic on a square of aluminum foil and pour 1 tablespoon olive oil over each head. Wrap the garlic up, totally sealing inside. Rotate in the Deep Basket for 45 minutes or until the garlic is very soft. Serve plain, squeezed out onto slices of bread or in recipes as directed.

BALSAMIC ONIONS

Serves 4.

4 medium onions, peeled
4 tablespoons olive oil
2 tablespoons balsamic vinegar
2 teaspoons dried thyme
Salt and pepper

Place onions on 4 large squares of aluminum foil. Drizzle with olive oil and vinegar; sprinkle with thyme, salt and pepper. Wrap each onion to totally enclose. Rotate in the Deep Basket for 45 to 60 minutes. Cut in half to serve or chop and serve.

ROASTED GARLIC POLENTA
WITH ROASTED VEGETABLE SALSA

Serves 4.

4 cups water
1 cup yellow cornmeal
1 teaspoon salt
1 head roasted garlic
1 tablespoon butter
2 tablespoons Parmesan cheese,
freshly grated
2 tablespoons olive oil

ROASTED VEGETABLE SALSA:
1 onion, quartered
1 red bell pepper, quartered
2 jalapenos, whole
3 tomatoes, seeded and chopped
2 tablespoons minced fresh cilantro
1 tablespoon olive oil
1 teaspoon fresh lime juice
Salt and pepper to taste

Bring water to boil in a large saucepan. Slowly
whisk in the cornmeal and add the salt.
Continue stirring over low heat until very thick
and cornmeal is cooked, about 10 to 15
minutes. Squeeze the roasted garlic into the
Polenta and stir in, along with butter and
Parmesan cheese. Pour into a lightly buttered
13 x 9 inch pan. Cool and then cover and
refrigerate for 3 hours or longer, until cold and
firmly set.

To make the salsa, place the onion, red bell pepper, and jalapenos in the Standard Flat Basket and rotate for 15 to 20 minutes or until tender. Cool slightly and coarsely chop. Stir in the tomatoes, cilantro, olive oil, lime juice, salt and pepper.

Cut the Polenta into large squares and brush with olive oil. Rotate the Polenta in the Standard Flat Basket with the basket facing the heat for 5 minutes on each side. Remove and serve topped with Salsa.

ROASTED TERIYAKI PORTABELLO MUSHROOMS

Serves 4.

4 medium Portabello mushrooms
Teriyaki Ginger Marinade (see page 215)

Trim the stems from the mushrooms and using a spoon, scrape out the dark brown gills on the underside of the mushrooms. Prepare the Marinade and add the mushrooms. Let stand for 30 to 60 minutes.

Remove mushrooms from the marinade and place in the Flat Standard Basket. Rotate for 20 minutes or until the mushrooms are tender. Serve as a side dish or in a bun for a sandwich.

MARINATED ROASTED RED PEPPERS

Serves 4.

3 red bell peppers
1/2 cup olive oil
3 tablespoons balsamic or red wine vinegar
1 tablespoon minced shallots
1 tablespoon Dijon mustard
Salt and pepper

Cut the peppers in half and remove the seeds and membrane. Rotate in the Flat Standard Basket for 15 to 20 minutes with the skin side facing the heat element, until blistered and blackened. Remove peppers and place in a paper bag for 10 minutes. Peel off the skin and cut into thick strips.

Make the marinade by combining the oil, vinegar, shallots, mustard, salt and pepper in a jar. Shake well to combine. Pour over the peppers and let stand at least 1 hour before serving.

CORN ON THE COB WITH HERB BUTTER

Serves 4.

4 ears fresh corn
1/2 cup butter, softened
1 green onion, minced
1/4 cup minced fresh parsley
1/2 teaspoon dried tarragon
1/2 teaspoon dried marjoram
1/8 teaspoon freshly ground black pepper

Soak the corn in the husks in cold water to cover. Place the corn in the Deep Basket and rotate for 20 minutes or until corn is hot through.

To make the Herb Butter, mash together the butter, green onion, parsley, tarragon, marjoram and pepper. Serve corn with Herb Butter.

ROASTED FRESH BEETS WITH ORANGE SAUCE

Serves 4.

1/3 cup fresh orange juice
1/3 cup chicken broth
Zest of 1/2 orange
1/2 teaspoon minced fresh rosemary
or 1/8 teaspoon dried rosemary
Salt and pepper to taste
1 tablespoon unsalted butter
8 fresh beets, peeled and ends trimmed

In a small saucepan combine the orange juice, chicken broth, orange zest, and rosemary. Bring to a boil, stirring often until reduced by about half. Season with salt and pepper.

Place the beets in the Deep Basket and rotate for 45 minutes or until very tender. Reheat the Orange Sauce and whisk in the butter. Pour over the beets to serve.

ACORN SQUASH WITH MAPLE GLAZE

Serves 4.

1 medium acorn squash
1/2 cup pure maple syrup
2 tablespoons butter
1/4 teaspoon ground ginger

Cut ends off the squash and cut into 4 equal thick slices. Cut out the seeds. Rotate in the Flat Standard Basket for 30 minutes or until tender.

Meanwhile, heat the maple syrup, butter, and ginger in a small saucepan. Serve squash topped with Maple Glaze.

ZUCCHINI PARMESAN

Serves 6.

6 small zucchini, cut into 1-inch chunks
1/4 cup butter
2 cloves minced garlic
1/2 cup freshly grated Parmesan cheese

Rotate zucchini in the Flat Standard Basket for 20 to 25 minutes or until tender. Meanwhile, melt butter with garlic in a small saucepan. Toss garlic butter with rotated zucchini and sprinkle with Parmesan cheese.

ROASTED SWEET POTATO WEDGES

Serves 3 to 4.

**2 large yams or sweet potatoes, peeled and
cut into quarters
2 tablespoons olive oil
1/2 teaspoon curry powder
Salt and pepper**

Prepare yams. Stir together the olive oil, curry powder, salt and pepper. Toss with potato wedges. Rotate potatoes in the Flat Standard Basket for 30 minutes or until tender when pierced.

GARLIC-ROSEMARY POTATO HALVES

Serves 6.

**3 medium russet potatoes, cut in half
lengthwise
2 tablespoons olive oil
1 clove garlic, minced
1 teaspoon minced fresh rosemary
Salt and pepper**

Place potatoes in Deep Basket. Stir together the olive oil, garlic and rosemary. Brush on the cut surface of the potatoes. Sprinkle with salt and pepper. Rotate the potatoes for 45 minutes or until tender when pierced. Brush with any remaining oil and serve.

HERBED NEW POTATO SKEWERS

Serves 6.

**2 pounds tiny red potatoes
1/4 cup olive oil
2 cloves garlic, minced
1 tablespoon mixed dried herbs**

Toss the potatoes with olive oil, garlic, and herbs. Thread the potatoes on the kebob skewers and rotate for 20 to 30 minutes or until tender.

LINGUINE WITH PEPPERS AND ONIONS

Serves 4.

**2 red bell peppers
2 medium onions
1 cup whipping cream
1 pound spinach linguine,
cooked and drained
1/2 cup freshly grated Parmesan cheese**

Cut peppers in half and remove seeds and membranes. Peel onions and cut in half crosswise. Rotate peppers and onions in the Flat Standard Basket for 20 minutes or until very tender. Remove and chop coarsely. Heat whipping cream in a medium skillet. Add the roasted peppers and onions. Simmer for 4 to 5 minutes. Add the cooked linguine and toss to coat well. Top with Parmesan cheese .

PASTA WITH ROASTED SUMMER VEGETABLES AND FETA CHEESE

Serves 4.

**1 zucchini, sliced in half lengthwise
1 small eggplant,
peeled and cut in half lengthwise
1 red onion, cut in half crosswise
1/4 cup olive oil
2 cloves garlic, minced
2 tablespoons minced fresh basil
1/2 pound bow-tie pasta,
cooked and drained
2 medium tomatoes, seeded and chopped
1/2 cup crumbled feta cheese**

Prepare the vegetables. Stir together the olive oil, garlic and basil. Brush the vegetables with a light coating of the oil mixture. Rotate the vegetables in the Deep Basket 20 minutes or until very tender. Remove and coarsely chop.

Toss vegetables with hot cooked pasta, the remaining oil mixture, tomatoes and feta cheese. Serve immediately.

ROTISSERIE & BBQ
Recipe Collection

DESSERTS

ROTISSERIE
&BBQ

Recipe Collection

FRUIT KEBOBS
WITH GRAND MARNIER GLAZE

Serves 12.

**1/2 fresh pineapple, peeled, cored and cut
into 1-inch wedges
4 bananas, cut into 1/2-inch slices
4 oranges, peeled and sectioned
12 large strawberries
1 cup sugar
1 teaspoon cinnamon or to taste
6 tablespoons Grand Marnier**

Thread the fruit evenly onto Kebob Rods, alternating pineapple, bananas, and oranges and placing one strawberry on the end of each.

Mix sugar and cinnamon and sprinkle over fruit. Rotate the skewered fruit for 15 to 20 minutes or until fruit is cooked through and lightly browned. Remove skewers from the gear wheels and slide the fruit off onto serving plates. Sprinkle each serving with 1 tablespoon Grand Marnier and serve immediately.

PINEAPPLE WEDGES WITH BROWN SUGAR SAUCE

Serves 4.

1 fresh pineapple
4 tablespoons butter
4 tablespoons brown sugar
2 tablespoons dark rum (optional)

Peel the pineapple and cut into eighths lengthwise. Cut off the core. Place the pineapple spears in the Flat Standard Basket. Rotate the pineapple for about 10 minutes or until warmed through and lightly browned.

Meanwhile, melt the butter and brown sugar in a small saucepan over medium heat. Add the rum, if desired, and stir to combine well. Drizzle the glaze over the hot pineapple and serve two spears per person.

BAKED CINNAMON APPLES

Serves 4.

4 medium apples
1/4 cup brown sugar
2 tablespoons toasted walnuts,
finely chopped
1/2 teaspoon ground cinnamon
1 tablespoon butter
Whipped cream

Core apples to within 1/2-inch of the base, leaving the bottoms intact. Cut off the stem top to fit back into the top of the apple.

Combine the brown sugar, walnuts, cinnamon and butter and pack into the apple. Fit the stem end back into the top. Rotate in the Deep Basket for 30 to 40 minutes or until apples are tender. Serve topped with whipped cream.

PEARS WITH BUTTERSCOTCH SAUCE

Serves 4.

**4 large firm ripe Anjou or Bartlett pears
3 tablespoons fresh lemon juice
2 tablespoons granulated sugar**

**BUTTERSCOTCH SAUCE:
1/3 cup evaporated milk or whipping cream
2 tablespoons brown sugar
2 teaspoons unsalted butter
1/2 teaspoon vanilla**

Peel the pears, halve them lengthwise and core. Toss with the lemon juice and granulated sugar. Rotate in the Flat Standard Basket for 30 minutes or until tender. Remove to serving bowls and top with Butterscotch Sauce.

To make sauce, combine the evaporated milk or cream, brown sugar, butter and vanilla in a small saucepan. Cook over medium heat, stirring constantly, until the mixture comes to a gentle boil. Cook until the sauce is smooth and slightly thickened, about 2 minutes.

BANANAS ROYALE
WITH CHOCOLATE SAUCE

Serves 4.

4 firm ripe bananas, unpeeled
Whipped cream

CHOCOLATE SAUCE:
1/2 cup light or heavy cream
2 tablespoons sugar
1 tablespoon unsalted butter
4 ounces semisweet chocolate, finely chopped
1 teaspoon vanilla

Pierce the bananas in 4 places. Rotate in the Deep Basket for 15 to 20 minutes or until very soft when pierced. Carefully peel and place on serving plates. Top with Chocolate Sauce and whipped cream.

To make sauce, heat the cream, sugar and butter in a medium saucepan to a rolling boil. Remove from heat and immediately add the chocolate. Let stand for a minute and whisk until smooth. Stir in the vanilla. Serve warm or cold.

BANANAS WITH RUM SAUCE

Serves 4.

4 bananas, unpeeled
2/3 cup brown sugar
1/2 cup fresh lime juice
1/4 cup dark rum
1/4 teaspoon ground nutmeg
1/4 cup toasted coconut

Pierce the bananas in 4 places. Rotate in the Deep Basket for 15 to 20 minutes or until very soft when pierced. Carefully peel and slice on the diagonal into 1/2-inch slices.

In a medium saucepan, combine the brown sugar, lime juice and rum. Stir in the cinnamon and nutmeg. Add the bananas and toss to coat with the sauce. Spoon into bowls to serve topped with toasted coconut.

TOASTED POUND CAKE WITH STRAWBERRIES AND CREAM

Serves 6.

6 1-inch thick slices pound cake
1/4 cup melted butter
2 baskets strawberries, sliced
3 tablespoons granulated sugar
Whipped cream

Rotate the pound cake slices in the Flat Standard Basket for 10 minutes or until toasty and warm. Remove to serving plates and top with sugared strawberries and whipped cream.

ROTISSERIE & BBQ

Recipe Collection

MARINADES

Recipe Collection

ORANGE-SOY MARINADE

Makes about 1/3 cup.

**2 tablespoons soy sauce
2 tablespoons orange juice concentrate
1 tablespoon lemon juice
1 tablespoon ketchup
1 clove garlic, minced**

Stir together all the ingredients and use to marinate chicken or fish fillets.

LEMON-GARLIC MARINADE

Makes about 1/3 cup.

**1/4 cup fresh lemon juice
1 tablespoon coarsely chopped garlic
1 tablespoon minced chives
or green onion tops**

Stir together all the ingredients and use to marinate chicken or fish fillets.

ASIAN-CITRUS MARINADE

Makes about 1/3 cup.

2 tablespoons fresh orange juice
1 tablespoon fresh lemon juice
1 teaspoon Hoisin sauce
1/2 teaspoon hot sauce
1 teaspoon finely minced fresh ginger
2 cloves garlic, minced

Stir together all the ingredients and use to marinate chicken, pork tenderloin, shrimp or fish fillets.

RASPBERRY MARINADE

Makes about 1 cup.

1 (12 ounce) jar seedless raspberry
preserves
3 tablespoons raspberry vinegar
or red wine vinegar
1/2 cup ketchup-style chili sauce
1 teaspoon Dijon mustard

Combine all ingredients in a small saucepan and bring to a boil. Lower heat and simmer 2 minutes. Cool. Use to marinate chicken, pork, or spareribs.

TROPICAL FRUIT MARINADE

Makes 1 cup.

1 mango, peeled and cubed
1/2 cup fresh orange juice
2 tablespoons fresh lemon juice
2 tablespoons olive oil
1/4 teaspoon dried thyme

Puree the mango with the orange juice, lemon juice, olive oil and thyme. Use to marinate chicken, shrimp and firm fish fillets.

TROPICAL RUM LIME MARINADE

Makes about 1/3 cup.

1/4 cup fresh lime juice
2 tablespoons dark rum
2 tablespoons vegetable oil
1 clove garlic, minced
1/8 teaspoon ground allspice
Pinch red pepper flakes

Combine the ingredients and use to marinate chicken, pork, or shrimp.

LIME-CHILI MARINADE

Makes about 1/2 cup.

1 (4-ounce) can diced green chilies
1 green onion, minced
1/4 cup fresh lime juice
1 tablespoon minced fresh cilantro

Stir all ingredients together and use to marinate
a whole roasting chicken, chicken breasts,
shrimp or fish fillets.

JAMAICAN JERK MARINADE

Makes about 1 cup.

1/4 cup chopped fresh cilantro
2 tablespoons finely minced fresh ginger
1/4 cup fresh lime juice
1/4 cup olive oil
1/4 cup dark rum
1/4 cup light brown sugar
1/4 cup soy sauce
2 teaspoons hot sauce
1 teaspoon ground nutmeg
1/2 teaspoon ground allspice
1/2 teaspoon ground cinnamon
1/4 teaspoon salt

Combine all ingredients and marinate pork,
chicken or shrimp.

CUBAN MOJO MARINADE

Makes about 3/4 cup.

1/4 cup olive oil
3 tablespoons fresh orange juice
3 tablespoons fresh lime juice
6 cloves garlic, minced
1 serrano chili, minced
1/2 teaspoon ground cumin
1/2 teaspoon slat

Combine all ingredients and use to marinate chicken or pork.

RED WINE AND HERB MARINADE

Makes about 1 cup.

1 cup dry red wine
1/4 cup chopped onion
1 clove garlic, minced
1 teaspoon minced fresh parsley
1 teaspoon fresh thyme leaves
1 bay leaf
1/2 teaspoon salt
1/4 teaspoon freshly ground black pepper

Combine all ingredients and use to marinate beef.

BEER MARINADE
WITH ONIONS AND SAGE

Makes 2 cups.

**1 (12-ounce) can beer
1 large onion, sliced
2 cloves garlic, minced
2 tablespoons sugar
1 teaspoon dried sage leaves
1/2 teaspoon salt
1/4 teaspoon freshly ground pepper**

Combine all ingredients and use to marinate steaks, pork or chicken.

KOREAN MARINADE

Makes 3/4 cup.

**6 green onions, finely chopped
5 cloves garlic, minced
1/2 cup soy sauce
2 tablespoons vegetable oil
2 tablespoons brown sugar
2 tablespoons dry sherry
1 tablespoon toasted sesame seeds
1/4 teaspoon freshly ground pepper**

Combine all ingredients and use to marinate beef or ribs.

TERIYAKI GINGER MARINADE

Makes about 1 cup.

1/2 cup soy sauce
1/2 cup dry white wine
1/4 cup sake or dry sherry
1/4 cup sugar
2 slices fresh ginger root
2 tablespoons water
1 tablespoon cornstarch

Combine the soy sauce, wine, sake or sherry, sugar and ginger in a small saucepan. Bring to a boil and then simmer over medium heat 3 minutes. Blend water with cornstarch; stir into sauce. Stir over medium heat 1 minute or until thickened. Strain sauce. Makes about 1 cup. Set aside to cool or refrigerate up to 1 week. Use as marinade for chicken, beef, pork or seafood.

HONEY DIJON MARINADE

Makes about 1/2 cup.

1/4 cup Dijon mustard
1/4 cup honey
2 tablespoons vegetable oil
Salt and pepper

Mix ingredients and use to marinate chicken.

THAI CILANTRO CHILI MARINADE

Makes about 1/4 cup.

1 bunch cilantro
6 cloves garlic, peeled
3 tablespoons fish sauce
2 tablespoons sugar
2 tablespoons vegetable oil
1/2 teaspoon freshly ground white pepper

Cut the top off the bunch of cilantro and place in the food processor. Add the garlic and pulse to finely mince. Add the remaining ingredients and puree. Use to marinate shrimp or chicken.

SAUCES

ROTISSERIE
&**BBQ**

Recipe Collection

TOMATO BBQ SAUCE

Makes 3 cups.

**2 tablespoons vegetable oil
1 medium onion, chopped
3 (8 ounce) cans tomato sauce
1/2 cup red wine vinegar
1/2 cup brown sugar
2 tablespoons Worcestershire sauce
1/2 teaspoon freshly ground pepper**

Heat oil in medium saucepan and sauté onion until softened. Stir in remaining ingredients and simmer, uncovered, until thickened, about 30 minutes, stirring occasionally. Let cool, then cover and refrigerate for up to 2 weeks.

CHIPOTLE BBQ SAUCE

Makes 1-1/2 cups.

3/4 cup ketchup-style chili sauce
1/3 cup molasses
3 tablespoons fresh lemon juice
1 tablespoon soy sauce
1 tablespoon dark brown sugar
1 tablespoon minced canned
Chipotles in adobo sauce
2 teaspoons Worcestershire sauce
1 teaspoon Dijon mustard
1/4 teaspoon red pepper flakes
1/2 fresh Anaheim chili, in 1-inch cubes
1/4 green bell pepper, in 1-inch cubes
1 clove garlic, minced
Salt and pepper

Combine 1/2 cup water with all ingredients in a heavy saucepan. Bring to a boil over high heat. Reduce heat to low and simmer uncovered, stirring occasionally, for 15 minutes. Remove sauce from heat and strain, pressing through as much of the sauce as possible; discard the solids. Let cool.

BOURBON-ORANGE BBQ SAUCE

Makes about 1-1/2 cups.

1/4 cup vegetable oil
1 large onion, minced
2/3 cup Bourbon
2/3 cup ketchup
1/2 cup cider vinegar
1/2 cup fresh orange juice
1/2 cup real maple syrup
1/3 cup dark molasses
2 tablespoons Worcestershire sauce
Salt and pepper

Heat oil in a large saucepan. Add onions and cook for about 10 minutes or until golden. Add remaining ingredients and bring to a simmer, stirring frequently. Reduce heat to low and cook until mixture thickens, about 40 minutes. Use as a glaze or continue to simmer until very thick and use as a serving sauce for pork or chicken.

HOISIN BBQ SAUCE

Makes about 1 cup.

**1 cup Hoisin sauce
2 tablespoons dry sherry
2 tablespoons Oriental sesame oil
1 tablespoon sugar
1-1/2 teaspoons rice vinegar**

Combine all ingredients and use to glaze chicken, pork or ribs.

MAYONNAISE BBQ SAUCE

Makes about 1-1/4 cups.

**1 cup mayonnaise
5 tablespoons prepared BBQ sauce**

Stir the BBQ sauce into the mayonnaise and use to brush over roast chicken.

CRANBERRY BASTING SAUCE

Makes about 1 cup.

**1 cup jellied cranberry sauce
2 tablespoons grenadine syrup
1/2 teaspoon hot sauce
1/2 teaspoon freshly ground pepper**

Place all ingredients in a medium saucepan and heat over medium-low heat to melt the cranberry sauce. Use to glaze turkey or chicken during rotating.

SPICY HONEY LEMON BASTING SAUCE

Makes about 1/2 cup.

**1/4 cup fresh lemon juice
1/2 teaspoon chili paste with garlic
1/2 cup honey**

Dissolve chili paste in lemon juice and stir in honey until blended. Use to glaze salmon or chicken.

CUMBERLAND SAUCE

Makes about 1-1/2 cups.

**Peel of 2 oranges, removed
with a vegetable peeler
Peel of 1/2 lemon, removed
with a vegetable peeler
1 cup fresh orange juice
1/4 cup fresh lemon juice
1 cup white wine
1 cup currant jelly
1 teaspoon dry mustard
1/2 teaspoon powdered ginger
1/2 teaspoon salt
Pinch cayenne pepper
1 tablespoon cornstarch
in 2 tablespoons water**

Combine orange and lemon peels with juices in a medium saucepan. Bring to a boil and simmer until peels become translucent, about 20 minutes. Strain, returning the liquid to the saucepan. Stir in the wine, jelly, mustard, ginger, salt and pepper. Bring to a boil and then simmer for 30 minutes. Add cornstarch mixture and boil 1 minute. Use to glaze poultry or as a sauce over rotated chicken or game hens.

CHERRY BRANDY SAUCE

Makes about 1-1/2 cups.

**1 (8 ounce) can pitted, dark sweet cherries,
reserve liquid
2/3 cup chicken broth
1 small onion, quartered
8 whole cloves
1/4 teaspoon ground cinnamon
1 tablespoon cornstarch mixed with
1 tablespoon water
2 tablespoons Brandy
1 tablespoon fresh lemon juice
1/4 cup grated lemon zest
Salt and pepper**

Place cherry liquid, broth, onion, cloves and cinnamon in a medium saucepan and bring to a boil. Cook, uncovered for about 8 minutes or until onion is tender. Strain liquid and discard onion pieces.

Return juices to the saucepan and stir in the cornstarch mixture. Bring to a boil, stirring often. Stir in cherries, Brandy, lemon juice and zest. Heat just to a simmer. Season to taste with salt and pepper. Use sauce over rotated poultry or pork.

Recipe Collection

SOUTH AMERICAN
CHIMICHURRI SAUCE

Makes about 1 cup.

**1/2 cup olive oil
1/4 cup red wine vinegar
1 small onion, finely chopped
1/3 cup finely chopped fresh parsley
4 cloves garlic, minced
1 tablespoon finely chopped fresh oregano
Salt to taste
1/4 teaspoon cayenne pepper
1/4 teaspoon freshly ground black pepper**

Whisk together the olive oil and vinegar. Stir in the onion, parsley, garlic, oregano, salt, cayenne and pepper. Let stand at room temperature for 2 to 3 hours before serving over steak.

THAI RED CURRY SAUCE

Makes about 1-1/2 cups.

1 tablespoon vegetable oil
2 tablespoons prepared Thai red-
curry paste
1 (14 ounce) can unsweetened
coconut milk
2 tablespoons fish sauce
1 tablespoon brown sugar
1/2 teaspoon salt
2 tablespoons minced fresh cilantro

Heat oil in a medium saucepan. Add curry paste and stir and mash into the oil over medium-low heat to warm the paste. Add the coconut milk and bring to a simmer. Stir in the fish sauce, sugar and salt. Taste for seasoning and stir in the cilantro just before pouring over rotated chicken, beef or pork.

CILANTRO CHILI SAUCE

Makes about 1/2 cup.

**2 (4 ounce) cans diced mild green chilies
1/3 cup dry white wine
2 green onions, chopped
1 tablespoon fresh lime juice
1 cup packed cilantro
1/2 cup hot melted butter**

Combine chilies, wine, green onions and lime juice in a small saucepan. Bring to a boil and continue to cook until mixture is reduced by half. Cool about 5 minutes. Pour into a food processor or blender and puree. Add the cilantro and finely chop. With machine running, add the hot melted butter. Serve immediately over rotated chicken or vegetables.

MUSTARD DILL SAUCE

Makes about 2 cups.

1/2 cup sugar
1 cup fresh dill
1 cup Dijon mustard
1/3 cup white wine vinegar
1/2 cup mayonnaise
2 tablespoons vegetable oil

Combine all ingredients except oil in a blender or food processor. Blend until smooth. With machine still running add the oil, drop by drop until absorbed. Store covered in refrigerator. Serve with fish or shrimp.

GINGER-GARLIC DIPPING SAUCE

Makes about 1/2 cup.

2 2-inch pieces of peeled fresh ginger
3 cloves garlic, peeled
1/2 cup soy sauce
1/2 teaspoon hot sauce
1 teaspoon honey
1 teaspoon vinegar
2 tablespoons chopped cilantro leaves

Combine the ginger, garlic, soy sauce, chili sauce, honey and vinegar in a blender or food processor. Puree and then stir in the cilantro. Serve as a dipping sauce for chicken wings or shrimp.

ASIAN SWEET-SPICY DIPPING SAUCE

Makes about 1 cup.

**1 cup sugar
1/2 cup water
1/2 cup white vinegar
1/2 teaspoon salt
2 teaspoons chili paste with garlic (or to taste)**

Combine sugar, water, vinegar and salt in a small saucepan. Bring to a boil, stirring until sugar dissolves. Reduce heat and simmer until syrupy, but do not allow sauce to caramelize, about 15 to 20 minutes. Remove from heat and stir in chili paste with garlic. Cool. Serve as a dipping sauce for chicken wings or shrimp.

PEANUT DIPPING SAUCE

Makes about 1-1/2 cups.

2/3 cup crunchy peanut butter
1-1/2 cups unsweetened canned
coconut milk
1/4 cup fresh lemon juice
2 tablespoons soy sauce
2 tablespoons brown sugar
1 teaspoon minced fresh ginger root
4 cloves garlic, minced
Pinch cayenne pepper
1/4 cup or more chicken broth

Combine the peanut butter, coconut milk, lemon juice, soy sauce, brown sugar, ginger, garlic and cayenne in a saucepan. Cook, stirring constantly, over medium heat, until the sauce is thick and fairly smooth, about 10 minutes. Pour sauce into the blender and puree, adding the chicken broth to thin as necessary. Serve with vegetables, pork or chicken.

APRICOT MUSTARD DIPPING SAUCE

Makes about 1-1/2 cups.

1-1/2 cups apricot preserves
6 tablespoons Dijon or Creole mustard

Combine the apricot preserves and mustard in a small saucepan over low heat. Heat gently, stirring often until the preserves melt. Stir to combine with mustard. Cool. Serve as a dip for spicy foods like the Cajun Chicken Wings.

CITRUS HORSERADISH SAUCE

Makes about 1 cup.

1 cup orange marmalade
2 tablespoons fresh orange juice
2 tablespoons fresh lemon juice
1-1/2 teaspoons prepared horseradish
1 teaspoon minced fresh ginger
1 teaspoon dry mustard

Combine all ingredients in a blender or food processor and puree. Store in refrigerator. Use as a sauce with spareribs, ham, pork, or shrimp.

ROTISSERIE & BBQ

Recipe Collection

RUBS

ROTISSERIE &BBQ

Recipe Collection

SPICY TEXAS RUB

Makes 3/4 cup.

6 tablespoons paprika
2 tablespoons ground black pepper
2 tablespoons chili powder
2 tablespoons salt
2 tablespoons sugar
1 tablespoon garlic powder
1 tablespoon onion powder
1-1/2 teaspoons cayenne pepper

Combine all ingredients and store in a jar for up to 6 months.

BBQ RUB

Makes 3/4 cup.

1/4 cup paprika
1 tablespoon ground cumin
1 tablespoon brown sugar
1 tablespoon chili powder
1 teaspoon garlic powder
1 teaspoon salt
1/2 teaspoon cayenne pepper
1/2 teaspoon freshly ground pepper

Combine all ingredients and store in a jar for up to 6 months.

CAJUN-CREOLE RUB

Makes 1/2 cup.

**2 tablespoons paprika
1 tablespoon garlic powder
2 teaspoons dried thyme, finely crumbled
1/2 teaspoon dried oregano,
finely crumbled
1 teaspoon cayenne pepper
1 teaspoon salt
1 teaspoon freshly ground pepper**

Combine all ingredients and store in a jar for up to 6 months.

ITALIAN HERB RUB

Makes 1/2 cup.

**2 tablespoons dried basil, finely crumbled
2 tablespoons dried oregano, finely
crumbled
1 tablespoon dried thyme, finely crumbled
1 tablespoon dried rosemary, finely
crumbled
1 tablespoon dried sage, finely crumbled
1 tablespoon salt
1 teaspoon freshly ground pepper**

Combine all ingredients and store in a jar for up to 6 months.

TROPICAL SWEET SPICE RUB

Makes 1/4 cup.

1 tablespoon ground allspice
1 tablespoon ground nutmeg
1 tablespoon ground cinnamon
1 teaspoon ground cloves
1 teaspoon cayenne pepper
1 teaspoon salt

Combine all ingredients and store in a jar for up to 6 months.

SOUTHWESTERN RUB

Makes 1/2 cup.

1/4 cup paprika
1/4 teaspoon ground cumin
1/4 teaspoon dried oregano
1/4 teaspoon dried thyme
1-1/2 teaspoons salt
2 cloves garlic, minced
3 tablespoons olive oil

Combine all ingredients together in a small bowl to form a paste. Use with pork or chicken.

MOROCCAN HARISSA RUB

Makes 1/2 cup.

**3 to 4 fresh red or green jalapenos, seeded
and minced
2 cloves garlic, minced
1/4 cup canned crushed tomatoes
1/2 tablespoon ground cumin
1/2 tablespoon ground coriander
3 tablespoons olive oil
1 tablespoon fresh lemon juice
2 to 3 teaspoons dried red pepper flakes**

Combine all ingredients in a food processor
and mix well. Cover and refrigerate for up to 2
weeks. Use as is over chicken or beef, or mix
with mayonnaise or sour cream and use as a
garnish.

CARIBBEAN SPICE RUB

Makes 1 cup.

2 tablespoons vegetable oil
2 tablespoons fresh lime juice
1 small onion, chopped
1-1/2 tablespoons minced fresh ginger
3 cloves garlic, minced
2 jalapenos, seeded and chopped
2 tablespoons minced fresh parsley
1 tablespoon dried thyme
1/2 teaspoon dry mustard

Combine all ingredients in food processor and mix well, to form a paste. Use as a rub for roasted chicken pieces.

BASIL PESTO RUB

Makes 1 cup.

**2 cloves garlic, peeled
1 cup fresh basil leaves
1/2 cup fresh parsley leaves
3 tablespoons pine nuts
3 tablespoons Parmesan cheese,
freshly grated
1/2 teaspoon salt
1/2 cup olive oil**

Place garlic, basil, parsley, pine nuts, Parmesan cheese and salt in the food processor. Pulse to finely chop. With machine running, pour in the oil to make a paste. Keep refrigerated for up to 4 to 5 days.